AMY'S TIN TABERNACLE

VICTOR MAXWELL

Best wishes

Rom 8:31

AMY'S TIN TABERNACLE

Amy Carmichael and The Welcome

VICTOR MAXWELL

Amy's Tin Tabernacle
Amy Carmichael and The Welcome

ISBN: 978-0-9927219-0-9

Published by Books 4 Publishing
Printed in the UK

Welcome Evangelical Church
163 Cambrai Street,
Belfast,
Northern Ireland
BT13 3JH

www.welcomechurch.co.uk

CONTENTS

DEDICATION

This book is dedicated to all members and friends of The Welcome, who have served their LORD and Saviour faithfully over the past 125 years.

Foreword

This remarkable story of *'The Welcome'* cannot fail to cause its readers to stop and praise the Sovereign Lord for all His power and grace at work there over the past 125 years.

To quote from the book, *'Through their missionaries the fruitful branches of the Welcome Hall's influence took blessings of Gospel grace to thousands of people around the world'*. As we read of God using ordinary people to do extraordinary things in His service to extend the Kingdom, it offers a serious challenge to us all to re-appraise our own commitment to spreading the Gospel.

The narrative sets the scene of life in Northern Ireland over the years and provides a helpful background to the continuing life and work of *'The Welcome'*.

As a 'sister fellowship' – having the same founder, Amy Carmichael, we should like to express our joy and thanks to the Lord for the 125 years of witness given by those associated with *'Amy's Tin Tabernacle'*.

On behalf of The Dohnavur Fellowship, I warmly welcome this book with its powerful testimony to the work Amy Carmichael began so long ago.

Sura Carunia (President)
The Dohnavur Fellowship,
Dohnavur,
Tirunelveli District,
India.

Preface

The prophet Zechariah reminds us that we should not despise the day of small things. Of this the famous Charles Haddon Spurgeon said, "It is usually God's way to begin His great works with a day of small things." The Lord used the cry of the infant Moses to save a nation. A young slave girl was His servant to bring healing to the mighty Syrian General, Naaman. With a small stone David slew the mighty Goliath. Little is much when God is in it.

When God opened the teenage heart of Amy Carmichael one hundred and thirty years ago, no one could have imagined all that would be accomplished in the life of this young girl from the seaside town of Millisle, County Down. The missions she established in Ireland and in India more than a century ago still flourish to this day and the influence of her writings is beyond measure.

In this volume I have endeavoured to relate the early story of Amy's life and work in Belfast, which resulted in the founding of the Welcome Hall. I am indebted to Jonathan Clarke, pastor at The Welcome Evangelical Church, and to the former pastor, Eddie Young, for all their help in providing so much relevant information. I also thank our kind friend Sura Carunia, President of The Dohnavur Fellowship, for consenting to write the foreword for this book. Sincere thanks also to Dr Jacky Woolcock and Tahany Hanna of The Dohnavur Fellowship UK, for their help and encouragement. We are indebted to The Dohnavur Fellowship for their kind permission to quote from the works of Amy Carmichael and to CLC for the consent given to quote her poems from the book "Mountain Breezes".

As always, I am also grateful to my wife, Audrey, for her patience, scrutiny and encouragement in all my writings and to our daughter and son-in-law, Heather and Tom Knutson, for kindly agreeing to proof read the original manuscript.

I have read widely to provide the material for this book and tried to acknowledge sources where possible. If I have overlooked giving credit where it may be due, I apologise.

Amy Carmichael's life and writings have been a blessing to thousands. God has used her life to bless me. I trust you also will be blessed in reading this volume.

Victor Maxwell

CHAPTER 1

A Life-Changing Sunday

Strong gusts of an icy cold wind blew constantly along Belfast's Bedford Street and Dublin Road one Sunday morning in 1885. The two- and three-storey buildings on either side of the narrow thoroughfare created a virtual wind tunnel. Besides the stiff breeze, the grey skies and low clouds overhead gave an ominous hint of impending rain. It was not a nice day. Pedestrians, holding their Edwardian hats or clutching their cloaks and umbrellas, leaned into the wind as they picked their way along the muddy street towards the nearby Shaftesbury Square while horse-drawn carriages transported more affluent citizens down the centre of the road.

Most of those on foot were smartly clad churchgoers returning home from their place of worship. Amongst them was the Carmichael family who were making their way home to 21 College Gardens, near to Queens University, after attending the morning worship service at Rosemary Street Presbyterian Church. The recently widowed Mrs Carmichael and her seven children would not normally have worried too much about the inclement conditions. They knew that soon they would be sitting down for a sumptuous meal and afterwards they would huddle around the fireside with their recently bereaved family members. David Carmichael, the family's devoted father and prominent businessman, had died on 12th April 1885 after a short illness.

The luxuries and comforts which the Carmichael's enjoyed in the prestigious home did not cloud or blur the eye of eighteen year-old Amy Carmichael. She spied a pathetic old woman who was bent over and carrying a heavy bundle as she slowly staggered along the street. The Carmichael family instinctively stopped in their tracks when they saw the pitiful lady. Until then they had undoubtedly been enjoying a lively conversation about the preacher's sermon topic, which was still fresh in their mind. However, the sight of this poor woman bent over her heavy bundle arrested their attention immediately.

The unknown lady's tattered and threadbare clothing, flapping like feathers in the wind, made her stand out in blunt contrast to the many well-dressed churchgoers who ignored the plight of the poor woman and passed her by on either side. Amy, the oldest of the Carmichael children, and her family pitied the unknown lady because of her evident signs of poverty, and they noticed that the pathetic soul was obviously struggling to carry the heavy bundle of unknown contents which were wrapped in a dirty bag. She had probably been gathering sticks or pieces of coal for a fire in an attempt to heat her home or perhaps scraps of food she had scavenged in the city centre.

Whatever the contents of the bundle, it was of no concern to Amy. She was more struck with the distress of the poor wretch, and instead of continuing on her homeward journey Amy summoned the aid of her two brothers to help the struggling lady. By this time the rain clouds opened and the persistent wind caused the cold rain to be driven horizontally into their faces. Nevertheless, the brothers gently relieved the woman of her heavy load and then put their arms under those of the lady and helped her along the street.

While Amy's youthful brothers used their physical strength

to help the elderly woman, Amy tenderly spoke words of comfort and Christian compassion to her. At the same time Amy became very conscious of the glares of disdain and contempt from some fashionable and religious passers by who were shocked to see three respectable teenagers associating with a pauper in such a public manner. Although they looked on quietly, yet it was obvious that they disapproved of the affluent Carmichael children stooping below their dignity to accompany this lowly woman on a public thoroughfare on a Sunday morning.

At first the demonstrative disapproval of the onlookers caused Amy to blush with embarrassment. She felt her face go crimson. Nevertheless, she and her brothers discounted the censure of the Victorian church-going public and continued with their mission of mercy to help this humble woman.

The three teenagers progressed slowly along the street until they came to a newly erected sandstone fountain at the junction of Dublin Road, Bedford Street and Ormeau Avenue (the sandstone figure still stands at the same location and just outside the headquarters of the BBC in Northern Ireland).

In spite of the persistent wind and driving rain Amy gazed at the fountain, and as she did so it was as though she heard an audible voice calling out of the greyness of that dull morning and saying to her, "Gold, silver, precious stones, wood, hay, stubble; every man's work shall be made manifest for the Day shall declare it, because it shall be tried by fire, and the fire shall try every man's work of what sort it is. If any man's work abide…"

This was a Bible quotation from 1 Corinthians 3:12-14 which Amy had undoubtedly memorised previously, but God brought them to her mind that morning and through them gave her a life-changing experience.

Amy impulsively turned to look into the greyness of surrounding buildings to see where the voice might have come from. Through the driving rain she could only see the muddy street and the passing people and nothing else. Amy did not speak to anyone about what had happened to her. She felt it was too personal, too intimate and too sacred; however, that Sunday morning incident not only changed her life, thereafter it changed her attitude to life's values and nothing would ever be the same again.

Even though Amy had been born into a privileged and prosperous family, from that moment onwards, she determined in her heart to forgo indulging in living for the wood, hay and stubble of selfish and secular pursuits and invest her life in reaching for the gold, silver and precious stones in service for her Saviour. Perhaps her longing heart was best expressed in a hymn that came into her possession at that time:

Upon a life I did not live
Upon a death I did not die,
Another's life, Another's death,
I stake my whole eternity.

Later, one of her brothers related that when the family eventually arrived home that Sunday afternoon, Amy shut herself into her room where on her knees she talked with God and settled once and for all the future pattern of her life. By her actions that day Amy had already embarked on her long missionary career.

There is no doubt that Sunday morning experience was pivotal in Amy Carmichael's young life. She was only seventeen. It may be said that everything that had happened in her previous years up to this stage had prepared her for that defining day, a day in which her eyes were opened to the real and eternal values of living for

God. That same day would also propel her into a life of dedicated service for God in which only eternal values would really matter.

The outcome of Amy Carmichael's life-changing experience on a Belfast street that Sunday morning would result in loyal and dedicated service for Christ which would transform thousands of people from near and far for decades to come and ultimately for eternity. At the same time, the compassion that motivated the actions of the three Carmichael teenagers that Sunday morning had deep roots which reached far back into Amy's past.

Amy Carmichael

CHAPTER 2

Looking at the Roots

The Carmichael family descended from traditional Scottish Covenanter stock that had originally arrived in Ulster from Ayrshire, Scotland in the middle of the eighteenth century. They settled in County Down where Amy's enterprising great-grandfather leased two flourmills in Millisle, a small seaside village on the east coast of the Ards Peninsula, three miles from Donaghadee and seven miles from Newtownards. One mill was powered by steam while the other by a waterwheel driven by the current of flowing water from a nearby dam, in the middle of which was a small island. This mill on the small island reputedly gave the village its name, Mill-isle.

Besides setting up their prosperous flourmills and providing employment for many families in the surrounding countryside, the Carmichael family was dedicated to their Saviour and to the witness of the Gospel in their neighbourhood. In 1773 the family built the Millisle Presbyterian Church and in the same year gave ground at the opposite end of the village for the erection of the Ballycopeland Presbyterian Church. Both of these churches continued as separate congregations for 130 years until the diminishing numbers at the Ballycopeland church constrained the two congregations to amalgamate in 1906 and form one church, the Millisle and Ballycopeland Presbyterian Church, which continues to this day.

The two Carmichael brothers, David and William, managed

the mills through the mid-nineteenth century. Those were the changing and challenging years of the British Industrial Revolution when foreign grain was being imported to Ireland through the nearby port of Donaghadee.

Such was David Carmichael's dedication to the success of the family business that he did not marry until he was thirty-seven years old. His bride was Catherine Jane Filson, the daughter of a leading and well-respected doctor from the fishing village of Portaferry, which is located on the southern tip of the Ards Peninsula.

The newly-weds set up their home in Millisle, and their first child, Amy Beatrice Carmichael, was born in the village on 16th December 1867. Although she was born in 1867 her birth was not registered at the Ballycopeland Presbyterian Church until 1868. Over the next decade David and Catherine Carmichael's home was blessed with six more children. In all, the Carmichael family was completed and well balanced with three girls and four boys.

In the same year that Amy was born the Carmichael's contributed a large sum of money to build a school on the opposite side of the street from the mill. Although this was an investment for the children in Millisle, Amy and her brothers and sisters were initially educated by several private governesses who taught them through their early elementary education. The nearby school continued to function in the same building until 1959 when Millisle's growing population demanded larger educational premises. The old school house still stands on Millisle's main street and today the site is the home of Millisle Baptist Church.

Amy and her siblings were not only reared by godly parents, but from infancy they were well versed in the Westminster Shorter

Catechism and the Holy Scriptures, which were taught at home and at the Ballycopeland church. Although the family home no longer stands today, we can well imagine that the old house once rang with the laughter, singing, scolding and shouts of the seven vibrant Carmichael children from that bygone age. That home held the history and early secrets of Amy Carmichael's life and future ministry.

Perhaps one of her earliest spiritual lessons came to Amy when she was only three years old. Observing that her mother's eyes were blue while hers were brown, Amy set about praying that the Lord would change the colour of her eyes to be blue like those of her mother. She was greatly bewildered on the next morning when she woke up to find that her eyes were still brown and not blue, as she had asked of the Lord.

Later in life Amy remembered this childhood incident and admitted that it taught her that when we pray, God, at times gives us what we ask for, but on other occasions He either delays in answering, or as was the case with changing the colour of Amy's eyes, God's answer was, "No."

Through this Amy learned that God always knows what is best and His ways are always perfect.

This incident probably was one reason that blue was Amy's favourite colour throughout her life. However, when she arrived in India she discovered that her brown eyes helped her identify and integrate with the Indian ladies. It was then that she was glad God had denied her request in that childish prayer and had not changed her brown eyes to blue.

From her earliest years Amy manifested her potential for

leadership, even if it involved leading her brothers and sisters in childish escapades, which sometimes horrified her mother and father. Perhaps because of the influence of competing with her two young brothers, Amy became somewhat of a tomboy. She had little interest in playing with dolls or other such feminine playthings as other girls did. Although as a little girl she had a doll's house filled with miniature furniture and neatly decorated, she preferred to toss all the furniture out and fill the small house with moss where she could raise her beetles and earwigs.

Amy also preferred to indulge much of her playtime in impish and mischievous pranks or activities, which endlessly got her and her brothers into trouble. One such incident happened on a sunny day when Amy and her two younger brothers were playing at their garden gate. She reminded them that mother had told them not to touch the poisonous pods which hung invitingly from the beautiful laburnum tree in the garden. Amy perilously challenged her younger brothers, "Let's count how many pods we need to swallow before we die."

The two boys were prepared to challenge their older sister so all three of them set about digesting the bitter and toxic pods. Before long the children felt quite uncomfortable and concluded that they had eaten enough. They sat down under the tree and began to patiently wait to see what would happen next.

What did happen next incurred the wrath of an angry mother. When she discovered what her children had been up to she was horrified. Mother marched her three shamefaced children straight into the kitchen where she quickly prepared a dreaded potion known as "Gregory's Powder". The three culprits hated this medicine, but each had to drink a teacupful right to the last drop and still be polite and say, "Thank you," to their mother.

Having to swallow "Gregory's Powder" was sufficient punishment to cure those three guilty children of ever trying to swallow laburnum pods or any other toxic garden plants. The flowering tree must have remained as an annual reminder to them of that nearly fateful day.

The long sandy beach, which stretched along the seashore across the road from their home, was ideal for the children to run, play and expend their childish energies. Amy also loved to ride her pony up and down the sandy stretch along the shore. Theirs was truly a happy and prosperous Christian home and an idyllic childhood. Amy and her siblings had five cousins, Uncle William's children, who also lived in Millisle. When the two families got together there was quite a crowd of the Carmichaels. When the families filed into the church on Sunday mornings they swelled the congregation and occupied several rows of pews. During their childhood years the Rev John Beatty was their minister and had been since 1860. Uncle William Carmichael was the presenter for the congregation and led them in singing the Psalms.

The Carmichaels were a benevolent family and were well respected in the local community. Not only did they provide employment for many people, Mrs Carmichael also frequently provided cakes and food for elderly and poor folk in the village. Amy had great pleasure in taking a bowl of soup or a hot meal to some of these needy neighbours. She remarked how much she enjoyed seeing their old and crinkled faces widen out with a broad smile as they received another kind token from Mrs Carmichael. These little deeds of kindness undoubtedly influenced little Amy who would replicate so much kindness to multitudes of needy people in years to come.

Although the Carmichael children had private education from

various governesses, not all of these ladies left a good impression; however, Miss Eleanor Milne was an exception. All the Carmichael children loved Miss Milne, and she was virtually looked upon as another daughter in the family. Besides teaching them reading, writing and arithmetic, Miss Milne took time to teach the Scriptures to the children and tell them stories of the great reformers and heroes of Christian history. These historical accounts of great men and women of God made an indelible mark on Amy's memory, and the story of their lives and exploits remained with her for years to come.

The brother of the Rev John Beatty, their minister at Ballycopeland Presbyterian Church, came to spend some time in Millisle. He had been a missionary in India, and during one furlough he occupied a house next door to his brother's manse. During that year Mrs Beatty, the missionary's wife, often gathered the children together on Sunday afternoons and held them spellbound with graphic stories of life in India. It was reported that when the other children left, Amy frequently stayed behind and begged Mrs Beatty to tell her more about her work in India.

In her early teens Amy had to leave her beloved Millisle and the comforts of family life. She was sent to Marlborough House, a Wesleyan Methodist Boarding School in Harrogate, Yorkshire, England to complete her education. It was not easy for Amy to settle into the strict regime at the school. She missed the warmth of her home and the company of her siblings. Those few years were not a particularly happy time for Amy. However, in spite of being far from home Amy manifested her inbred leadership qualities in a mischievous and, at times, perverse way. On more than one occasion she led her fellow students into some unconventional activities, which landed them into some trouble and incurred the displeasure of the school's stern headmistress, Miss Kay.

Notwithstanding her unhappiness in being far from home, in 1883, when Amy was only fifteen years old and still a student at the Marlborough House Boarding School, she experienced a radical spiritual conversion. Mr Edwin Arrowsmith, an evangelist with the Children's Special Service Mission (CSSM) conducted services for the youth in Harrogate. Amy attended those meetings in the company of other students.

As Amy listened to Mr Arrowsmith's Bible lessons she heard again the familiar truths of the Gospel that she had learned as a child in Millisle. At the end of one of the meetings Mr Arrowsmith led the young people in singing the well-known children's hymn; "Jesus loves me this I know..."

After the service finished and other children began to leave Amy remained sitting in the quietness. She silently prayed, confessing her sin and received Jesus Christ into her heart. At that moment it seemed as though her soul flooded with a sense of God's love and presence. That day changed Amy Carmichael's young life forever.

Let the sea roar
and the waves
clap their hands

Millisle 1867-1883

Amy
Amy Carmichael
1867-1951

CHAPTER 3

A Crisis

Great changes had taken place in the Carmichael's family business back home in Northern Ireland during Amy's three-year absence from Millisle. Her dad and Uncle William had agreed that Uncle William should remain in Millisle to manage their two mills in the town while Amy's dad would move to Belfast to oversee a new mill that the Carmichaels had purchased at the Dufferin Dock in the city. With David Carmichael being assigned to manage this new enterprise he moved his family to a new home at College Gardens in Belfast's select Malone Road area.

Sadly, shortly after Mr Carmichael embarked on this new business venture he suffered some unforeseen financial and social reversals. He had loaned a considerable amount of money to a friend in need, but sadly, when the loan was due to be repaid the friend defaulted, and this left David Carmichael high and dry. It was thought that this financial crisis probably effected Mr Carmichael's health, which began to fail shortly after this incident. When it became obvious that their father's health was deteriorating the children were recalled from the boarding schools, Amy from Marlborough House and her two brothers from the King William College on the Isle of Man.

Mr David Carmichael died peacefully on 12th April 1885, almost nine months before Amy's eighteenth birthday. Her father's death had a profound effect on all the family, but especially on Amy. It seemed to accelerate her maturity, for Amy not only came of age, she also became more responsible at home and active in her Christian life and service. She engaged in helping people in poor neighbourhoods of the city. From the nearby streets Amy gathered boys and girls together and took them back to her home. There she taught them Bible stories and then gave them something to eat before they returned to their homes.

Although her formal schooling had been suddenly interrupted Amy continued studying subjects that were deemed to be most suitable for young ladies of her social standing: music, singing and painting. Along with her siblings she produced an in-house periodical, which they named, *The Scraps*. Each of the children had a pseudonym under which they recorded their devotional aspirations in poetry and prose.

Amy also established what she called "The Morning Watch". This involved a number of young people, including two of her brothers, who pledged to follow a course of Bible reading and prayer and then meet at her home on Saturday mornings to compare notes and pray together. Amy organised weekly prayer meetings for a group of girls in various homes. When the numbers attending these prayer meetings became too many for a house, some of the teachers at Victoria College invited Amy and her friends to conduct their weekly prayer meeting at the school.

At this time of spiritual growth and increasing zeal in Amy's life, she was introduced to Dr Henry Montgomery. This Presbyterian minister had a long association with the work and outreach of the Belfast City Mission and afterwards became the minister of Albert Street Presbyterian Church. The success of his ministry in Albert Street led to him founding the Shankill Road Mission, which began as an outreach from his church.

Henry Montgomery had been acquainted with the Carmichael family for some time. When he became aware of Amy's concern for the lost and the poor, he introduced her to another side of life on the back streets of Belfast on Saturday nights. Amy, who had led such a sheltered life until then, was touched and at times shocked, to see not only the poor social conditions of these areas, but also the ravages of sin and degradation on these underprivileged families. Amy discovered that added to their poverty, these people seemed to have little time for the Gospel or any concern for their soul's welfare. Their desperate plight made another indelible mark on Amy's young heart.

(It was around this same time that Amy and her brothers broke the ranks of Presbyterian respectability when they went to the aid of the poor old lady who was struggling to carry a heavy bundle along Belfast's Dublin Road.)

Amy soon struck up a friendship with Dr Montgomery's daughter, Eleanor, and, with the help of two other girls, they conducted a Monday evening Bible class for boys. At the same time, Amy started a Sunday morning Bible class at Rosemary Street Presbyterian Church for deprived girls, most of who worked in Belfast's busy linen mills. These girls did not enjoy the benefit of wearing respectable go-to-church Sunday clothes as did other young ladies of a more wealthy class. Instead of pretentious hats and fancy dresses, they covered their heads with grey or black shawls which they wrapped around their lower body to conceal their plain and sometimes threadbare apparel. For obvious reasons these lower class girls gained the nickname of "shawlies", distinguishing them from the upper class ladies.

Amy spoke to Dr Park, the minister at the Rosemary Street Presbyterian Church, about providing a room where she could teach the Scriptures to these underprivileged girls. Dr Park, always ready to try something new and unconventional, much to the shock of his parishioners, gladly consented to Amy's request and allowed her to use the Church Hall for her outreach. Although Amy's mother supported her in this evangelistic enterprise amongst the "shawlies", she was concerned for her daughter's welfare. Mrs Park, the minister's wife remarked to Mrs Carmichael, "I would let no child of mine go down those streets."

In September of that same year, 1886, when she started her work amongst the "shawlies", Amy was invited to visit Glasgow. While there she attended a meeting for the deepening of the Christian life, organised after the pattern of the recently established Keswick Convention. Amy had another impressionable and crisis experience as a result of that meeting although it seemed to be a most unlikely setting for a life changing experience.

A grey mist appeared to hang in the air while two preachers gave their addresses and Amy felt that the atmosphere of the meeting was dull and cold. Notwithstanding the external ambience, God spoke to Amy again, not as a result of the preaching, but in the chairman's closing prayer. In that prayer the man of God quoted Jude 24, "O Lord, Thou art able to keep us from falling."

Those words were like a shaft of all pervading light shining into Amy's soul. She realised her relationship with God was secured by the Lord Himself, for He was able to constantly keep her in His love.

From that meeting Amy returned to Belfast with a renewed confidence. Thereafter she was enabled to put her father's death behind her and dedicate her life to those eternal riches for which she longed.

More than two years after her father's death Mrs Carmichael called her children together into their dining room and told them that nearly all the family's finances had been lost. Mother invited them to kneel with her while she prayed and committed the matter to God. Amy had already proved that God and His grace were sufficient for her life and summed the situation up with, "He has been so kind about other things that we cannot doubt that He will care for this too."

Amy's conversion at the CSSM meeting in Harrogate; her experience at the water fountain on Belfast's Dublin Road when she heard God speak about living for the real values in life; the gold, silver and precious stones; the moment of consecration during the closing prayer at the Keswick meeting in Glasgow; all these played a vital part in moulding Amy to be the vessel God wanted her to be and would use so effectively in His work in years to come.

That work began on the streets of Belfast.

Belfast in 1890

CHAPTER 4

When Belfast Became a City

The latter half of the 19th century is generally acclaimed to have been Belfast's golden era. In 1888 Belfast was granted city status by Queen Victoria, and this made it the ninth largest city in the British Isles and Ireland's only industrial city. The economic boom in Belfast was largely due to the prosperous linen trade, the heavy engineering works, the tobacco factories and the world-renowned shipbuilding yards at Harland and Wolff. This company alone employed up to 35,000 workers and was one of the largest shipbuilders in the world. Because of the city's growing economy, migrants flooded into Belfast from across Ireland, Scotland, and England; also many came from the rural areas of Ulster.

This influx of workers caused Belfast's population to grow by 400% increasing from 22,000 in 1806 to nearly 340,000 by the end of the nineteenth century. Most of the workers employed in the linen mills, tobacco factories, engineering works and shipyards lived in row after row of small, red brick terraced houses which were built under the shadow of the places where they worked. It was not unusual for several members of the same family to be employed in the same establishment, and many of their small, two-up, two down, houses were often overcrowded with large families.

"Millies" was a condescending name given to mill workers while the nickname, "shawlies", was accorded to girls and women who covered their heads and upper body with a shawl. To see a woman with a black or grey shawl wrapped around her was not uncommon at that time.

Most of these workers toiled long hours, under harsh conditions for low wages and often, little respect. A workingman's wage was quite meager, but even less was paid for female and child labour which was very common at that time. A typical working day began at 6.30 a.m. To make sure the workers were not late for their work the factory horn sounded all over the immediate vicinity to waken them at 5.30 a.m. Those who did not arrive for starting time were generally locked out while the others worked through until 6.00 p.m. Too many late starts not only meant that wages were reduced but frequently resulted in dismissal from employment. On Saturdays the machines generally stopped at midday.

The city's industrial revival created a good life for the 'linen lords' and other entrepreneurs of that Victorian era. Many of them used their wealth to build magnificent villas on the outskirts of the expanding city in order to escape the worst of the grime and stench, which largely prevailed in the inner city.

The late 19th century also saw the growth of civic and academic establishments as well as an increase in scientific achievement. Northern Ireland's leading university, Queen's University, was formed in 1845. The magnificent Harbour Commissioners Office was built in 1854. The equally grand Custom House was built in 1857, and the Ulster Hall was built in 1862. The Albert Memorial Clock was erected in the city centre in 1869 in honour of Prince Albert, Queen Victoria's husband. The Marquis of Donegal built the ornate Belfast Castle in 1870. The Belfast Public Library and the Albert Bridge were built in 1890. The Grand Opera House was constructed in 1895. The busy St Georges Market was opened in 1896. Although the Ulster Museum dates from 1833 and the Botanic and Horticultural Society was formed in Belfast in 1827, they created the Palm House only in 1840, and the Botanic Gardens became a public park in 1895. From 1872 horse drawn trams trafficked through the streets of Belfast.

After Amy's visit to Glasgow in 1886 she returned to this expanding Belfast where she continued to work with a deep passion and great enthusiasm amongst her Belfast "shawlies". Soon her Sunday morning Bible class at the Rosemary Street Presbyterian Church Hall was not only packed to capacity, it was often overflowing with as many as four hundred of these mill girls crowding into the fashionable church. These girls might have been socially poor, but they were hungry for the Gospel and the Bible. Amy was totally consumed with imparting to them the Word of Life.

The increased numbers of these unrefined girls attending the stylish downtown church soon created an unwelcome and adverse disturbance amongst some church members. This was especially so when these uppity people heard some of these girls pray--sometimes more than one at the same time. Furthermore, besides being a little loud, these girls seemed to address God in their coarse and common vernacular, which the church members felt was unbecoming to Presbyterians. It must be said that many of these girls had no social skills. One of them for obvious reasons was colloquially nicknamed "Fighting Sal".

Several church people even stood watching the girls with folded arms and contemptuous expressions, which they could not conceal. These disapproving members finally made their objections known to Dr Park who had supported Amy throughout her endeavour to bring these girls to faith in Christ. However,

God, who makes the wrath of man to praise Him, used these unwelcome and discontented complainers so that, instead of hindering Amy's outreach amongst the mill girls, they would actually be the harbinger of a new work that God would unfold for Amy in the near future.

The unhappy church members were relieved when they learned that Amy and her friends were actively looking for an alternate location where she could accommodate her weekly Bible class without any harassment. She solicited prayer from her friends and the mill girls that God would provide their need and indicate a suitable place for them to meet. At the same time Amy was at a loss to know where the new location might be or how they would be able to afford to rent or purchase a building.

Just then someone drew Amy's attention to an advertisement in *The Christian*, a monthly publication, which was circulated around the churches at that time. The ad was offering the sale of a corrugated iron building, which reputably had the capacity for five hundred people and could be purchased for £500. The advertisement sounded like a Godsend, and Amy was so excited.

However, with the death her father the Carmichael family's assets had dwindled to virtually nothing and left Amy with no fixed income. Her depleted resources meant that she did not have the means to purchase this prefabricated building. At the same time, Amy remembered that when she was a child in Millisle she was asked to collect donations for the Bird's Nest, a Christian orphanage in Dublin. When she as a child had visited her grandmother in Portaferry she had taken her collecting card with her and had asked some of her grandma's friends and neighbours to contribute to the cause. One man who had recently built a new house flatly refused to donate anything to the fund. Amy had felt rebuffed and disappointed by this cold response and never forgot the incident. As a result of that experience Amy reasoned, "Why not ask God to speak to those who love Him and motivate them to help those whom He loves, rather than ask help from those who don't love God?"

Could it also be that Hudson Taylor, founder of the China Inland Mission, who had visited Belfast earlier that year, had influenced Amy to trust God to supply her needs? She had been challenged by his appeal for the lost in Asia, but also impressed by his testimony of the life of faith and the principle by which he worked, "God's work, done in God's way, will not lack God's supply."

Amy enthusiastically shared with her girls the vision God had given her to purchase this iron hall. Their burden of prayer thereafter was for God to meet this need and send them the £500 they needed.

In one of Amy's editorials in *Scraps*, the Carmichael's in-house publication, Amy had set out her attitude to the life of faith. She wrote at length about Moses and Aaron appealing to the Children of Israel to make their contributions for the building of the Tabernacle in the Wilderness. In her article she pointed out that Moses did not have a bazaar or a sale of work to raise funds for God's house. In her observations she quoted Exodus 35:22, "And they came, both men and women, as many as were willing hearted, and brought bracelets, and earrings, and rings, and tablets, all jewels of gold: and every man that offered offered an offering of gold unto the Lord."

From this verse and the surrounding context Amy established three principles when she was alone with God before her open Bible:

1. As many as were willing hearted gave of their substance.
2. They gave their own possessions.
3. They gave unto the Lord.

Based on this observation Amy reminded herself of the great promises of God; "The gold and the silver are mine..." (1 Kings 20:3), "Ask and you shall receive (John 16:24), "My God shall supply all your need" (Philippians 4:19). Armed with these and other great promises from God's Word, Amy established early in her Christian service some principles that would guide her for her future work at the Welcome Hall, the name she felt should be given to her new mission.

1. Is the work for which we want money God's chosen work for us or our chosen work for Him? If the former, will not He see to the money necessary? If the latter, then how can we expect anything better than what we have?
2. Can we expect a blessing to follow money given grudgingly?
3. Should we not see that our root is right, before expecting flowers and fruit? Amy did not depart from these early-established principles throughout the rest of her life.

One day soon after the girls began to pray for God to send in the funds, Amy and her mother were visiting in a friend's house. The hostess showed an unusual interest in Amy's work with the Belfast mill girls. Amy related how the work had grown, but as a consequence of this growth in numbers at the Bible Class some people were uneasy with the influx of these coarse mill girls.

One of Mrs Carmichael's friends told Amy and her mother that she knew of a lady who wanted to do something in memory of a friend who had died. This friend thought that to build a hall for the mill girls was the sort of thing the lady might be very keen to do.

Within a few days Amy received a letter from this unknown lady, Miss Kate Mitchell, the daughter of a wealthy linen baron who lived in Olinda, Craigavad, near to Bangor on the County Down coast. In the letter Miss Mitchell invited Amy to lunch at her home and said that she would like to know more about her work with the Belfast mill girls.

Before going to Olinda for that prearranged visit, Amy learned that although Miss Kate Mitchell was a lady of considerable means, she was also very zealous for the Kingdom of God. Even Amy, who was used to the trapping of wealth, was greatly fascinated with Miss Mitchell's charming and prestigious home. More than that, she was even more impressed to learn that Miss Mitchell had led all her servants to personal faith in the Lord Jesus Christ.

Amy travelled to Olinda and from the moment the butler opened the hall door and showed her in she was made very welcome at Miss Mitchell's opulent home. Amy later remarked that Miss Kate Mitchell was like a white violet flower, God's white violet.

Lunch was served in a sunny room, which over-looked a charming and colourful garden. The table was covered with an immaculately laundered white tablecloth and rich silverware set for two people. During lunch Miss Mitchell enquired from Amy about the mill girls. Amy answered as best she could without any sense of begging she told Miss Mitchell of the burden on her heart for these girls, the growth of the work and their pursuit for a suitable place to meet.

A few days after her visit to Olinda Amy received another letter from Miss Mitchell to say that she wished to give the money to buy the iron hall. This was a great answer to prayer, but Amy and her friends faced another daunting challenge; with the expanding industry and housing in Belfast, land was very valuable, and it would be very difficult to secure a place near one of the big mills and in the heart of the district where most of Amy's girls lived.

Encouraged by the fact that God had already answered prayer in providing the money to purchase the hall, Amy challenged her girls to pray that God would also make a suitable building site available for them. It was then that someone suggested to Amy that faith without works is dead and that she should take steps to make sure that their prayers were answered by going to speak with the Director of Ewart's, the biggest mill in that part of Belfast, and ask him how much he would charge for a site for their prefabricated hall.

At first Amy hesitated to face the owner of the mill with such an audacious enquiry. However, God had already honoured their faith, and she was sure He would do the same again. Before Amy left the great man's office, Mr Ewart had readily agreed to rent a piece of land on the corner of Cambrai Street and Heather Street for a very nominal fee. Cambrai Street runs from the top of the Shankill Road through to the Crumlin Road. Morrison's, a grocery shop occupied the site at that time and the adjacent Heather Street had not yet been named as it had only recently been designated as a new development. The location was perfect.

Amy decided that they would call her corrugated tin hall, "The Welcome". The name was most appropriate for this new venture in view of the reproach she and her friends had experienced from more affluent churchgoers in trying to reach the derided mill girls.

CHAPTER 5

Opening The Tin Tabernacle

There was great excitement amongst Amy's mill girls when they learned they had secured a place where they could erect their own hall right in the middle of the district where they lived. Attending Amy's Bible class at the Rosemary Street Church had been a great blessing to them, but they also were aware that their presence at the downtown church in such great numbers had caused some embarrassing problems. With the new hall on the Shankill there would be no more embarrassment. Their simple tin hall bore two simple words above the door, which would never embarrass anyone: The Welcome.

This new undertaking, however, was not without its critics who disdainfully labelled the hall as "The Tin Tabernacle". Notwithstanding these critics, the prefabricated iron hall was duly erected on the site, and the mill girls were happy to help decorate their new building and make curtains for the windows.

Belfast solicitors, W. & D. Johns, supplied the conveyance of the property and prepared the title deeds for the original six trustees of the Welcome. The trustees were, Miss Kate Mitchell, Dr Henry Montgomery, Mr Samuel Johnston, Robert Barclay Pim, Elias Hugh Bell and Amy's mother, Catherine Carmichael. It is interesting that Amy did not become a signatory to the trust deed. Perhaps she was envisaging her future service beyond the work at the Welcome Hall. At this time she was not yet twenty-two years old.

The erection of the hall was completed in good time. Invitation leaflets were printed and sent out to many people for the opening of The Welcome on 2nd January 1889. Amy's invitation leaflet described the new hall as being the mill and factory girls branch of the YWCA with which Amy had been associated for a few years. The underlying reason for opening the Welcome Hall was perhaps reflected by a little composition Amy included on the inaugural invitation:

Come one. Come all.
To the Welcome Hall
And come in your working clothes.

Right from the beginning the Welcome Hall was neutral ground, for there was no distinction by social class. The "shawlie" girls felt just as much at home as Amy's family and her more affluent friends who freely mingled with and sat beside the mill girls attending the meetings. Miss Mitchell, the original donor, travelled from her splendid residence at Olinda to mix with girls she might not have met if it had not been for her acquaintance with Amy and her involvement in purchasing the building for the Welcome Hall.

Dr Park, Amy's minister at Rosemary Street Presbyterian Church, who had withstood the criticism of his flock about the presence of the mill girls at their church, remained a great encouragement to Amy as she embarked on this mission to reach the "shawlies". For that reason Amy invited Dr Park to speak at the dedication service for the new building. Although Amy sat on the platform during that opening service, her eyes were fixed on the hand-painted text that she had requested should be displayed on the wall above the low platform: "That in all things He might have the pre-eminence" (Colossians 1:17). When she rose to speak Amy simply said, "As truly, as truly I knew how, I wanted those words to be fulfilled."

Now, 125 years later, those same words are still prominently displayed above the platform at The Welcome Evangelical Church: "That in all things He might have the pre-eminence." That motto has been a continuing guide to the Christ-centred ministry of the Welcome Hall.

The dedication of the Welcome Hall was followed by a two-week evangelistic campaign conducted by two of Dwight L. Moody's evangelists from the USA. Besides preaching alternatively each night the two evangelists introduced a new hymn to the friends at the Welcome:

I know not why God's wondrous grace
To me He hath made known,
Nor why unworthy as I am
He chose me for His own.

But I know Whom I have believed,
And am persuaded that He is able
To keep that which I've committed
Unto Him against that day.

It was at these meetings that this well-known Gospel hymn was sung for the first time in the British Isles, and instantly it became a favourite with all who attended the Welcome. In the weeks that followed, the lively tune of this new hymn was being whistled or sung on the streets around the newly constructed hall, although the tune did not always conform to the original melody that the

Americans had taught. Amy used to wince when she heard some of the girls sing out of tune at the top of their voices. She could not help think of what the folk back in the Rosemary Street church might have thought of the strange sounds and airs that were passed off as hymns of faith at the Welcome Hall.

Nevertheless, the blessings continued, and on each night during those first weeks many souls were introduced to the Saviour.

Amy testified later that the blessing flowed every night until on a certain night she discerned a dryness and hardness in the meeting. No one had been converted on that night. She was perplexed and wondered why and where the power of God had gone. Years later Amy wrote, "There is nothing dreary or doubtful about (the Christian life). It is meant to be continually joyful... We are called to a settled happiness in the Lord whose joy is our strength." However, on this occasion Amy was very sensitive to the Holy Spirit's promptings, and as she searched her heart she felt that in all the celebration and excitement at the Welcome, they had become too jocular and light. She sought forgiveness for grieving the Spirit in this way, and very soon the blessing returned to the evangelistic services.

After the inaugural evangelistic meetings the enthusiastic congregation at the Welcome Hall settled down to a busy weekly schedule.

Sunday	4:30 p.m.	Bible Class
	5:30 p.m.	Sunbeam Band Meeting
Monday	7:30 p.m.	Singing Practice
	1:20 p.m.	Dinner Hour Prayer Meeting
Tuesday	7:30 p.m.	Night School
Wednesday	7:30 p.m.	Girl's Meeting

	1:20 p.m.	Dinner Hour Prayer Meeting
Thursday	4:00 p.m.	Mother's Meeting
Friday	1:20 p.m.	Dinner Hour Prayer Meeting

This was a great work and a heavy responsibility for a young girl of twenty-two years to sustain. Besides the weekly routine of meetings Amy was also active in attending to the social needs of people in the area. She did not always have the means to buy what the people needed, but she trusted God to supply the wherewithal, and He did.

Amy also organised bands of girls to go with her to help the aged in the side streets of the Shankill. She also trained and involved them in taking on active parts in the meetings at the Welcome, although she always spoke at the Sunday Gospel service.

In later years Amy wrote of the Welcome with very fond memories, "Every foot of that place is dear to me. Everything concerning it was prayed over... I never forget the Welcome and my beloved girls." However, Amy did not stay at *The Welcome* for long.

With the family's straightened financial circumstances Amy's two oldest brothers went to America, and later the two youngest would also immigrate, one to Canada and the other to South Africa.

Within a year of opening the Welcome a long standing family friend, Mr Jacob Wakefield MacGill, invited Mrs Carmichael and her daughters to go and live in Manchester. He wanted Amy to carry on a work amongst the factory girls at Ancoats in the same way that she had done at the Welcome.

While her mother worked as the Superintendent of a Rescue Home associated with Star Hall, a mission outreach that was also in Ancoats, Amy rented a room near to her Manchester *Welcome*.

Sadly, her work in Manchester was cut short when Amy became ill due to overwork and poor living conditions. For convalescence Amy travelled to the residence of Mr Robert Wilson, another family friend who had previously invited Amy and her family to Keswick in 1888. In the process of her frequent visits to Mr Wilson at Broughton Grange, Amy was virtually adopted as a daughter in his family.

Other fields still beckoned for Amy. Several years after dedicating her life for missionary service abroad at the Keswick convention, Amy departed England in March 1893 on the P&O SS Valetta bound for Japan. She was sent as one of the first missionaries from the Keswick movement to work under the direction of Rev Barclay Buxton who was a close friend of Mr Robert Wilson.

During the next fifty years of her missionary career she did not return again to the Welcome or to her native Northern Ireland.

During her year in Japan Amy worked herself into exhaustion and because of ill health had to return to England. This was a difficult period in her life, but another door soon opened for Amy. In 1895 she applied to the England Zenana Missionary Society and was accepted for the work in India where she worked for some time with the much-respected missionary, Mr Thomas Walker of Tinnevelly.

It was in India that Amy founded the renowned and highly esteemed work of the Dohnavur Fellowship. This work was established to reach and rescue many of the exploited "temple children," the abused and neglected waifs that lived on India's streets. Like her work among the "shawlies" in Belfast, the mission to the needy street urchins grew rapidly and became very effective and efficient.

On 4th October 1931, Amy suffered a major health crisis and subsequently was confined to bed for the rest of her life. From her bedroom Amy directed the work of the Dohnavur Fellowship, and with her enforced seclusion she put her pen to good use. She wrote letters of encouragement to many of God's servants and authored thirty-five books, many of which are considered to be Christian classics. Her devotional writings are well known all round the world. Amy Carmichael passed away in 1951.

Relating to an encounter she had with a waif while still in Belfast, Amy composed a little doggerel for her family paper, *Scraps*, which not only was so simple in view of her greater literary talents, but it also expressed her deep concern for the poor and the lost:

When I grow up and money have,
I know what I shall do.
I'll build a great and lovely place
For little ones like you.

Amy Carmichael realised that dream when she and her friends built a beautiful rescue home for hundreds of India's children. She also left a large imprint on Belfast's Shankill Road when she built the Welcome as a rescue centre for lost souls.

God's work is always greater than any of His workers and even though Amy Carmichael had departed from the Welcome and the streets of Belfast, God still had a great future for that work.

Come one Come all to the Welcome Hall
and come in your working clothes

The Welcome

Shankill 1885-1889

Amy

CHAPTER 6

Passing On the Reins

After Amy's departure from the work of the Welcome, Miss Kate Mitchell, the generous donor who had purchased the original building, stepped in to take on the leadership of the work. She received a lot of encouragement from Dr Henry Montgomery who was the honorary secretary of the Belfast City Mission for more than forty-six years. With great energy, vision and passion, Dr Montgomery was building up a growing evangelical work amongst the people on the lower Shankill Road and was keen to see the witness at the Welcome Hall continue.

In the summer of 1896 Dr Montgomery erected a large tent on what was to be the future site of the Shankill Road Mission. He conducted a seven-week evangelistic mission for the working people of the general neighbourhood, and crowded congregations heard the Gospel every night. The mission proved so successful that the tent mission continued for almost a year. By then hundreds of people had been converted to Jesus Christ.

In 1898 Dr Montgomery left his ministry at Albert Street Presbyterian Church to open The Shankill Road Mission where he provided help for the poor, free medical treatment, free second hand clothing and Christian education. These were very radical and unconventional measures at that time, but they did help to reach the masses with the Gospel of Jesus Christ.

A sense of spiritual revival prevailed amongst the mill and factory workers of the Shankill Road area. Miss Mitchell could not let the torch of Gospel witness that Amy had ignited, fade out or lapse into dying embers. Although she had not been endowed with the same gifts and abilities as Amy Carmichael, yet she gave herself whole-heartedly to the work at the Welcome. There is no doubt that she had been inspired by young Amy's zeal for the Saviour and her passion for the work.

Miss Mitchell was glad that the Trustees of the Welcome had rallied around to support her as she applied her time and freely used her means to help the needy and reach the lost with the Gospel on the upper Shankill area. This was a big step for Miss Mitchell who travelled more than twenty miles several days each week from her home in the leafy village of Olinda so that she could continue in the work amongst the mill girls on the Shankill. Many of these girls had been trained by Amy and were skilful in leading the meetings and even speaking at the various services. They also gave the same loyal devotion to Miss Mitchell as they had previously shown to Amy.

One evening in May 1902, while returning from another day of serving her Lord on the Shankill, Miss Mitchell succumbed to a pulmonary infection and after a short illness she went to be with the Lord whom she had served so well. Miss Mitchell's death was a watershed and the end of an era. While many felt indebted to her, sadly, with her demise the interest and leadership of the work at the Welcome waned, and very soon, in the early years of the twentieth century, the Trustees had to make a hard decision: either to try to carry on with the fledging work or to close down this Gospel witness on Cambrai Street.

Although at the turn of the new century Belfast's linen and manufacturing industries were still prospering, yet this prosperity did not filter down to the workers, and very little was done to improve the social conditions for the masses of people who lived in the tightly compacted streets of the inner city. However, the great 1859 revival, which swept across Ulster fifty years earlier, was still making a great spiritual impact on the population. Dr Montgomery's work on the Shankill was still being greatly blessed by God, and every week over a thousand people crammed into the Mission's Albert Hall.

Added to this, in 1903, the American evangelist, Reuben A. Torrey and his song leader, Charles Alexander, conducted a month-long evangelistic crusade in the city. It was during these services that Dr Alexander introduced his new hymnbook, Alexander Hymn's No.3. Every night Dr Torrey preached soul-stirring messages from the Bible, and at the end of every service multitudes of people accepted Jesus Christ as Saviour. It seemed as though the fires of the '59 revival were being fanned again. This spiritual resurgence under the preaching of the renowned evangelist caused the numbers of people attending the evangelistic services to increase every night to the point that there was not a church in the city that was big enough to accommodate such a large gathering. Due to this dilemma the organisers of the Torrey/Alexander crusade decided to conduct the final week of meetings at the newly constructed St George's Market. With this new venue more than seven thousand people were able to attend each night of the final week and hundreds of these were converted.

As had been the case with Amy's work more than a decade earlier, many of the converts were 'millies', 'shawlies' and common factory workers. The great impact of those meetings was manifested on the city's streets when groups of mill girls sang Dr Alexander's hymns as they walked to work before 6.00 a.m. in the morning. Others started cottage prayer meetings in their homes. It was an ironic and sad contrast that at this time of spiritual renewal in Belfast coincided with the slow and sad demise of the work at the

Welcome Hall. Although the work at Amy's Tin Tabernacle had begun with great evangelistic zeal, that early fervour diminished with the passing of Miss Mitchell until the premises were soon being used more for social and educational purposes instead of the purposes for which it was founded. No longer was the Word of God read and preached from the low platform nor did the rafters resonate with the animated singing of the sometimes out-of-tune mill girls. Instead, the premises were being used for sewing classes and demonstrations of commercial items. These had taken the place of the initial evangelistic enthusiasm that had been demonstrated under Amy's leadership.

The Welcome, which had once been a burning and shining light on the Shankill, now lay idle. Its flame and influence had been extinguished. It was a sad reversal and a painful decision, but the Trustees felt they had no alternative other than to disband the work.

For the next twenty-six years Amy's corrugated iron premises, constructed with so much eagerness and sacrifice, were used for various social activities and commercial enterprises. For some years Finlay's Soap & Candles, a Northern Irish company with headquarters at Victoria Square in Belfast's city centre, used the hall as a deposit for their goods. The large sign, which had been displayed outside the Welcome inviting people to the meetings, was replaced with a plaque announcing the virtues of using Finlay's Soap. Inside the hall Amy's inscription above the old platform could still be seen on the wall, "That in all things He might have the pre-eminence." Sadly, for the next quarter of a century, other things would have the pre-eminence. The early zeal that had built the Tin Tabernacle and established the Welcome vanished, and the once open doors were now tightly shut. Was that the end of the Welcome? Had Amy's dream died? Were Miss Mitchell's ten years of labours and sacrifice all been in vain?

CHAPTER 7

The Johnston Revival

During the first twenty-five years of the twentieth century Ulster and the rest of Ireland were convulsed in political mayhem and public turmoil. The Ulster Unionists and Irish Nationalists were poised for civil war with each other over the imposition of the Home Rule Bill, which the British Government introduced in 1912. The Unionists believed that this Home Rule Bill would undermine the Union between Great Britain and Ireland. The Unionist resistance was led by Edward Carson and in spite of his followers' staunch loyalty to the Crown, they resolved to withstand the Bill in every way possible, lawfully or otherwise.

On 'Ulster Day', September 28th, 1912, Carson, led a massive public gathering of almost 500,000 people to publicly declare their opposition to the Home Rule Bill by signing the Ulster Covenant, a declaration in which they stated that they would use 'all means which may be found necessary' to defeat the Bill and defend the Union.

Consequently, by 1913 ninety thousand volunteers joined the Ulster Volunteer Force (UVF), a newly formed paramilitary force drawn from the Unionist population. These volunteers avowed their readiness to seize strategic locations across Ulster to support a provisional government and were even prepared to fight the

British military to secure and maintain their British citizenship. They went so far as to import arms to reinforce their cause and determination. In reaction to this the fledgling UVF was soon rivaled by another movement; The Irish Volunteers. This republican movement recruited an even greater number of nationalists to counterbalance the threat of the UVF in Ulster.

When the Home Rule Bill was about to become law in 1914, Edward Carson rallied the UVF combatants and declared, "Now, men, that you have got your arms, no matter what happens, I rely upon every man to fight with those arms to the end."

By the conclusion of the summer of 1914, many of the men from both of these volunteer paramilitary organisations would indeed be at war and losing their lives, but not in a conflict with each other. Thousands of these men, from all over Ireland, joined different divisions of the British Army to fight against a common enemy when the United Kingdom went to war against Germany in what was known as "The Great War", which was supposed to be "the war to end all wars".

Many of these volunteers came from the tightly packed streets of the Shankill Road and the Crumlin Road. They had given up their employment in the mills and factories, left their heartbroken families and marched off to war. Many of these men never returned home again. They fell as casualties of the Great War.

After months of training during 1914 and 1915, the Ulster Divisions arrived in France in late 1915. They soon found themselves in the Somme area, but were not initially fighting side by side. On 1st July 1916, the first day of the Battle of the Somme, the brave men of the 36th Ulster Division engaged the German enemy with devastating results. Disregarding their own safety, they 'went over the top' and suffered terrible casualties. In two days, out of a total of about 15,000 men, 5,500 of them were killed, wounded or missing.

After the conclusion of World War I in 1918 many of the surviving and war-weary soldiers returned to their native Ulster only to find that Ireland was again plunged into civil and political upheaval. The brutal conflict of the Irish War for Independence raged from 1919 through to 1922. This was immediately followed by the Irish Civil War of 1922-1923, which resulted in the partitioning of Ireland and the establishment of Northern Ireland, six of Ulster's Counties, which opted to remain part of the United Kingdom.

It is quite ironic that while Ulster was engulfed in so much civil and political chaos, God using a most unorthodox, but a mighty preacher of the Gospel to stir the winds of revival in Belfast. His name was William Patterson Nicholson. W. P. Nicholson, who had been converted as a rough seaman, spoke the plain vernacular of the Ulster people. Under his fiery preaching hundreds were converted, especially on the Shankill Road.

In 1922, Dr Henry Montgomery, who had established the work of the Shankill Road Mission more than twenty years earlier, invited Mr Nicholson to conduct an evangelistic mission at the Albert Hall. This was the first of many great evangelistic crusades Mr Nicholson would conduct in various parts Belfast. This first Nicholson mission brought fresh spiritual impetus and a sense of revival to the Shankill Road.

Alas, through all those years of civil turmoil, political wrangling and repeated wars the witness at the Welcome Hall had remained silent. No voice from the pulpit at the Welcome was heard in the community. Those doors, once wide open for people to hear the Gospel, had stayed shut except for an occasional sewing class.

Instead of sowing the good seed of God's Word local girls were at the hall sewing their garments and instead of souls being saved at The Welcome the premises were used for storing soap.

This certainly was not what Amy Carmichael had in mind when she founded the work at the Welcome or what Miss Mitchell had given the final years of her life to maintain. However, in spite of this dereliction from its original purpose, God had His plan. God had His man for that hour of spiritual revival.

In 1926 Canon Warren, a godly rector at St. Silas Church of Ireland on the Cliftonville Road, was greatly concerned when he noticed the vacant and neglected Welcome Hall premises on Cambrai Street. He was even more disturbed when he learned of how Amy Carmichael's original vision for a work amongst the working class people of the area had been abandoned. Canon Warren was influenced by Amy's original vision and knew that this hall could be used to reach many people in this area with the Gospel. Furthermore, he had a man in mind, Jack Johnston from nearby in Leopold Street.

Jack Johnston was born in Tunney, Ballinderry in 1886. After leaving school he found employment as a textile engineer at the Combe Barbour & Combe Textile Engineering Works. To be nearer the factory Jack left his Ballinderry home in the country and lodged with one of his sisters, Mollie, in Palmer Street, which was also near to the neglected Welcome Hall. His apprenticeship in Belfast was during the time of Nicholson's spiritual revival in that neighbourhood, and consequently Jack Johnston was converted to Jesus Christ.

From the earliest days after his conversion Jack Johnston was out and out for his Lord. As a young Christian He unconditionally surrendered his everything to the Saviour and constantly yielded his will to serve the Lord and follow Him wherever He might lead. Jack's motto for maintaining his fellowship with God was from 2 Corinthians 5:9; "Wherefore we labour, that, whether present or absent, we may be accepted of him." Jack always wanted to be a workman approved of God and knew that for every Christian there would be a day when they would have to give an account to God of what they had done with their lives.

Another verse that helped regulate Jack's life was 2 Peter 3:14, " Wherefore, beloved, seeing that ye look for such things, be diligent that ye may be found of him in peace, without spot, and blameless." For that reason Jack Johnston used to say, "I try to keep short accounts with God." He also admonished others to do the same.

As a young man Jack cultivated his devotional life and became a man of prayer. He prayed over the smallest decisions in his life and frequently quoted the maxim, "Much prayer, much blessing; little prayer, little blessing." It was obvious that the 'much blessing' on his life was attributed to his 'much praying'.

It was a marvellous answer to Jack's prayers when he met Miss Elizabeth Barrett McGee, a dedicated Faith Mission Pilgrim. He soon fell in love with her. Elizabeth was a gracious and gifted Christian worker, who like Jack, was also dedicated to serving the Lord Jesus Christ. Besides her obvious physical charm and attraction, Jack was greatly impressed and influenced by Elizabeth's spiritual calibre. As their relationship developed Elizabeth resigned from the Faith Mission and married Jack. Although they did not know what God had planned for their future, they combined their lives, pooled resources and talents and were available to be used in the Lord's service wherever He might indicate.

That commitment did not take Jack and Elizabeth far from home, but the impact of it would eventually be felt in distant places. The young couple initially set up their home in a small apartment above a nursery retail shop, which Elizabeth had opened on the Shankill Road. While Jack continued in his job at Combe Barbour & Combe Textile Engineering Works, Elizabeth worked in the shop below their apartment. In the evenings they were given opportunities to put their many talents to good use in the Lord's work at various meetings in west and north Belfast.

When Canon Warren first approached Jack about the neglected hall on Cambrai and its potential, Jack declined Canon's initiative. He said that he did not know any of the trustees, and therefore, would be hesitant about venturing into someone else's patch. However, when he later shared the Canon's suggestion with Elizabeth she had a different opinion and encouraged Jack to accept the challenge and give it a try.

Amy Carmichael would have agreed with Elizabeth Johnston for she believed that Christians should seize every opportunity to serve the Lord. Far off in India Amy had written, "Satan is so much more in earnest than we are--he buys up the opportunity while we are wondering how much it will cost."

CHAPTER 8

Reaching Out Into the Community

Although it seemed that the Welcome Hall's Gospel beacon, flamed and fired by the passion and zeal of Amy Carmichael and Kate Mitchell, had been extinguished, in actual fact, it was only smouldering. The reviving and reinvigorating of the Gospel witness at the Welcome began when a neighbour, Mrs Lowry, opened her home on Cambrai Street for a monthly Faith Mission Prayer Union. Very soon the numbers attending that cottage prayer meeting outgrew the capacity of Mrs Lowry's small terrace house and another venue was needed.

Mr McClean of the Faith Mission, who had known Miss Kate Mitchell, asked permission from the Trustees of the Welcome to conduct a monthly Prayer Union in a small room at the rear of the Cambrai Street Hall. When the trustees gave their consent Mrs Lowry was very happy with the move to the Welcome. Mr McClean and Mrs Lowry did not know at that stage that the Lord was already touching the hearts of His servants, Jack and Elizabeth Johnston, to re-establish the Gospel witness at the Welcome.

Once Mrs Lowry learned how the Lord had spoken to Jack and Elizabeth Johnston, she whole-heartedly supported them in their endeavours to see the work of the Welcome Hall re-established in her neighbourhood. She prayed with them and for them.

The first thing Mr Johnston did was to start a weekly prayer meeting, a continuation of the Faith Mission Prayer Union. He had already learned the importance of dependence upon the Lord. The next step Jack took was to invite some local boys for a Bible Class on Sunday afternoons. This venture was an immediate success and became so well attended that several girls approached Mrs Johnston and asked if they could have a similar class at the Hall. Elizabeth readily agreed to their request on the condition that they would be able to bring together at least fifteen girls for the Girl's Bible Class. On the first Sunday seventeen young girls turned up at Elizabeth's class to learn more about the Scriptures.

This was the beginning of what would soon develop into a regular Sunday School which prospered and grew until there were so many children attending that Mr Johnston had to divide the Sunday School into many classes, each with its own dedicated teacher.

The small weekly prayer group, the Bible Class and Sunday School continued at the rear of the Welcome premises for more than a year. About that time a man who worked in the Springfield Road Post Office, challenged Mr Johnston, "Why don't you open the big doors at the front of the hall for a Sunday night Gospel meeting?"

At first Jack was hesitant. He told his friend that he thought the small room at the back of the hall was big enough for the present. However, the man insisted that the Lord would bless him if he took a step of faith and opened the doors to the general public. Mr and Mrs Johnston, always open to the Lord's prompting, and after much prayerful consideration, finally felt the man's challenge was the Lord's way of urging them to enter into a new phase of the Lord's work at the Welcome Hall.

The tide of blessing that had commenced with Nicholson's mission on the Shankill Road continued to have an effect on the wider community, and many local families were converted by the grace of God. Jack Johnston, filled with enthusiastic zeal, engaged in a soul-winning ministry in the pulpit and out of it. Preachers were invited to speak at the weekly evangelistic meeting at the hall.

Having now established the general Gospel meeting on Sunday nights, Jack and Elizabeth Johnston steadfastly continued in their mission to reach the lost for Jesus Christ among the upper Shankill community.

Besides his pulpit ministry, Jack seldom missed an opportunity to witness to the public of his faith in Jesus Christ. Sometimes he prayerfully approached passers-by on the street and politely asked them if they could answer a question for him. On agreeing to his request Mr Johnston posed this query by quoting 1 Peter 4:17, "If the righteous scarcely be saved, where shall the ungodly and the sinner appear?"

People were frequently startled at Mr Johnston's pertinent question, and few people could answer his question. It was then that Jack took advantage of the opportunity to discuss the individual's need of salvation through Jesus Christ.

On other occasions when travelling by train or coach with fellow Christians, Mr Johnston would purposely speak up with a raised voice and inquire from one of their party, "Tell me when and where you were saved." This was Mr Johnston's subtle ploy for his friend to answer with an equally raised voice and give his testimony to the unwitting passengers.

Jack Johnston was always alert to the need of the lost around him, and his passion was to seek to win them for Jesus Christ. Open-air meetings all over the Shankill area also played a big part in Mr Johnston's evangelistic endeavours. A team of Christians from the Welcome accompanied Pastor Johnston to sing and testify at these meetings.

Little by little the work at the Welcome began to grow. From the small weekly prayer meeting and a growing Sunday School there emerged the Sunday evening evangelistic service each week. Very soon there was a full compliment of meetings throughout the week with the addition of a Saturday Night Fellowship meeting and a Sunday morning Breaking of Bread Service.

These developments were fully supported by the Trustees who, at that time, were guided by Mrs Brownrigg of Seapatrick, near Banbridge, a niece of Miss Kate Mitchell.

From Jack Johnston's earliest days at the Welcome Hall he laid great emphasis on issues that were important in his own life: evangelism of the lost, holiness of personal life and full surrender to the will of God. There is no doubt that the growth of the hall was a reflection of these qualities in Mr and Mrs Johnston's lives.

He constantly exhorted the young people to be single eyed, keep one aim in view, the glory of God. On one occasion a lady asked Pastor Johnston if she could use the hall for a birthday party. "What will you be doing at it?" asked the pastor.

"We will only be having a bit of fun. There is nothing in it." The woman reassuringly replied.

The lady was taken aback when Mr Johnston answered, "That is exactly it. You can't have it for there is nothing in it." He had a single eye for the kingdom of God and truly believed the adage, "only one life will soon be passed. Only what's done for Jesus will last."

Jack Johnston used to encourage others to work for God in a little limerick he often quoted:

Do what you can, being what you are.
Shine like a glow-worm, if not like a star.
Work like a pulley, if you can't like a crane.
Be a wheel greaser, if you can't drive the train.

Within two years of embarking on his mission at the suggestion of Canon Warren, Jack became the pastor and superintendent of the work in the Welcome Hall. This was an honorary position for which he refused any salary or payment. Mrs Johnston's business at Johnston's Baby Shop on the Shankill Road provided the wherewithal for their daily living. Their service for the Lord at The Welcome was based on the same faith principles that Amy Carmichael had laid down at the outset of her work.

Jack went to great pains to make sure his character and motives were clean before God and men, a man of the utmost integrity. He preferred to miss out on a business deal rather than to have any suspicion of scheming or underhand dealings. That integrity was perhaps most evident when someone else was culpable of a fault or fell into some shortcoming. At such times the wise pastor showed the greatest discretion in helping to correct the errant individual and in order to protect the person he would quote the Scriptures, "Publish it not in Gath, nor the streets of Askelon lest the Philistines rejoice."

Pastor J. Johnston

CHAPTER 9

Missionary Enterprise

God truly used Jack Johnston in his evangelistic thrust, but He also used him to build up the church body at the Welcome Hall and send out workers to various mission fields. During Pastor Johnston's tenure he Welcome Hall sent out eleven missionaries to serve the Lord at home and abroad.

In the early days of Pastor Johnston's work a young man who had been converted during Mr Nicholson's Mission on the Shankill arrived at the Welcome one evening. His name was Jim Grainger, and his home was nearby on Cambrai Street. Jim later related that when he was seventeen years old, out of a sense of amusement, he went to hear Mr Nicholson preach at the Albert Hall one night in 1922. Jim had heard that this fearless Ulster preacher was quite outspoken and very unorthodox. However, rather than be amused by the preacher, the young man was captivated by Nicholson's powerful preaching and was overcome with a deep sense of his own sin and personal guilt. Jim was left in no doubt that night that he needed to be saved. However, even though God had spoken to him in the meeting, Jim had resisted God's promptings during the invitational appeal that night.

In spite of Jim's resistance to God and the Gospel, he was drawn back to Nicholson's meeting on another evening that week. Once again he experienced the same sense of need and an urge to respond to the evangelist's passionate appeal at the end of the meeting. Alas, Jim left the meeting as before without accepting Jesus Christ as Saviour.

Thankfully, the Holy Spirit did not withdraw from Jim. It seemed as though God was striving with him all that week. On Friday night of that same week Jim went back to the meeting at the Albert Hall. He said that although he smoked a cigarette on the way to the meeting, he knew that would be his last 'Woodbine' for he was determined to get right with God that night. When the Gospel appeal was made after Mr Nicholson had preached, young Jim Grainger was one of the first to respond to the appeal and in his heart say, "I will," to Jesus Christ. He returned home to Cambrai Street that night filled with the new-found joy of God's salvation and told his Christian parents that he had trusted Jesus Christ as Saviour. They were thrilled.

When Mr Johnston came on the scene to open the Welcome Hall in 1926 Jim Grainger was greatly enthused to learn that the hall was to be opened for a weekly prayer meeting. It was at the Welcome that Jim began to grow and mature in his Christian life, and under the tutelage of Mr Johnston he surrendered his all to Jesus Christ to receive God's fullness in his life and be prepared for whatever the Lord might choose for his future.

Right from the beginning Mr Johnston knew that this young man would not be with him at the Welcome Hall for long. Although he was very involved in helping Mr Johnston in the early days of the work Jim Grainger soon felt God's call on his life for missionary service. Following the revival under Mr Nicholson's evangelistic mission on the Shankill there most certainly was an unusual move of God amongst young men and women on the Shankill. Many of them were motivated to invest their lives for Jesus Christ and the furtherance of the Gospel.

Besides Jim Grainger being sent out into the work from the Welcome Hall to serve God in Africa, Joe and Mamie Wright, Fred Wright, Willie and Margaret McComb, Joe McComb and Mollie Harvey all went to the Amazon. Fred Wright and two of his colleagues were martyred by the Kayapo Indians on the River Xingu in 1935. Violet McGrath went to Japan. All of these young people were associated with Northumberland Street Mission Hall, which was adjacent to the Shankill Mission. Some of them, including Fred Wright, visited the Welcome Hall before they left for distant fields.

After a short period at the Missionary Training Colony, Jim joined the ranks of the Heart of Africa Mission (this later became the Worldwide Evangelisation Crusade) for their work in the Belgian Congo. For his first three years in Africa Jim worked alongside the great missionary, C T Studd, founder of the WEC. He remained with Mr Studd until the great missionary pioneer died in 1931.

Jim Grainger continued to work in the Belgian Congo for more than fifty-seven years and was highly respected by his missionary colleagues and national Christians. He and his wife Ida were still in the Congo during the terrible Zimba uprising of 1964 when many of their missionary colleagues were martyred in the rebellion.

On Wednesday, 27th July 1964, Jim and his wife Ida arrived home to their mission station in Yumbi. They immediately sensed a sinister apprehension among the people and missionaries. The country was in turmoil and rumours were rife of horrible atrocities that were taking place in some areas. On 24th August, a group of Zimba rebels arrived at their door threatening to kill them unless they did as the rebels commanded.

It was a stressful time, but for the next two months Jim and Ida continued in their work although it was always under a sense of duress. On 31ˢᵗ October 1964, at three o'clock in the morning, the Graingers were wakened by the sound of a car arriving outside their home. A few minutes later there was quite a demanding knock on their door. When Jim opened the door well-armed soldiers pushed by him and rushed into the house. The rebels demanded of Jim and Ida to handover their passports and accompany them to Punia, which was twenty-five miles away.

They were not allowed to take any baggage with them except for the clothing they were wearing, but Jim hid a small Bible in his pocket. It was a rough ride through the night, but when they finally arrived in Punia the dawn was beginning to break. The soldiers roughly escorted them from their vehicle and made them join a group of Belgian nationals. These men had been working in the diamond mines.

The rebels took the passports from all the hostages before herding all of them into the rear of another truck. They had another frightening trip for another one hundred and ten miles further south. Jim was aware that hundreds of people had been brutally killed by rebels along this road and was therefore a little apprehensive.

On arrival at this new location, Jim, Ida and nineteen other white foreigners were ushered into a building where they continued to be held captive. Soon they discovered that other nearby houses also held foreign white hostages. There were about seventy hostages in all.

Jim, Ida and their fellow hostages were held in captivity from Monday through to Thursday of that week. On that horrific day, 5ᵗʰ November 1964, all of the hostages except Jim and Ida were ordered to assemble outside where they were told that they would be shot.

The agitated crowd of locals on the street was obviously supportive of the rebels and they were also baying for the blood of Jim and Ida. Just when the situation seemed most hopeless, without a shot being fired and for no apparent reason, all the hostages were ordered back indoors again. The tearful and fearful group of Belgians were convinced that the rebels were only delaying the hour of execution.

At that crucial moment Jim appealed to the director of the Belgian miners, who was being held hostage with them, to call his colleagues together for a time of prayer. The director had no hesitation in complying with this request and soon had his men clustered around Jim. With his open Bible Jim began to read the comforting and reassuring words of the Lord Jesus in John 14:1-6; "Let not your heart be troubled. Ye believe in God, believe also in me..."

As he looked into the dejected faces of the despairing men around him, Jim knew that these poignant words were penetrating their hearts. He continued to explain to his captive audience how they could obtain forgiveness through Jesus Christ and then led them in a simple prayer of confession and repentance. Some of the men wept as they audibly repeated Jim's prayer. After this Jim encouraged his assembled listeners to ask God for deliverance from their precarious situation. He prayed again and then had all the men repeat the Lord's Prayer audibly.

Fifteen minutes after they had finished their devotional time, the subdued quietness was shattered by a sudden clatter of automatic gunfire. The rat-tat-tat of machine gun fire filled the air. Jim and Ida crouched low for cover and as they did so they could see some rebels fleeing for their lives. An exchange of gunfire continued for more than an hour during which the missionaries and miners continued to take cover. It was during this time that Jim and his friends were overjoyed to discover that a company of mercenary soldiers had arrived on the compound in the nick of time. Not only did Jim and his friends breathe a sigh of relief, they recognised that this was an undoubted and an immediate answer to their prayers.

The director of the Belgian miners was so delighted that he asked Jim to lead his group in a thanksgiving prayer to God for liberating them so soon after they had prayed. All the Belgian miners spontaneously fell to their knees and as tears flowed freely, Jim prayed. He afterwards reported that it was such a wonderful sight to see those hardened and irreligious miners weeping before God. They had been miraculously snatched from the virtual jaws of a cruel death.

Jim and Ida were eventually evacuated out of the war zone to Elizabethville. After the war both of them continued to serve the Lord in the heart of Africa for years to come. After completing fifty-seven years of faithful and fruitful missionary service for God in the Congo Jim went to be with Christ while he was still in harness.

Just prior to his home-going Jim visited Belfast for the last time. During that visit he attended a meeting in the Welcome Hall when a challenge was given for those present to dedicate their lives to the Lord afresh. Jim, although advanced in age and having spent over half a century in Africa, was the first on his feet, offering himself unreservedly to God. Within a week Jim Grainger was at home with his Lord.

He not only loved Africa, the Africans loved him. More than a thousand Congolese people attended his funeral service in Zaire. This Belfast lad had gone from the heart of the Shankill and from the Welcome Hall to serve God in the heart of Africa. The fruitful branches of Amy Carmichael's foundational work had surely spread far.

CHAPTER 10

Spiritual Moving and Social Depression

In the 1930s Belfast's local industries were badly affected by the global recession of the Great Depression. As a result, thousands of local workers were made redundant, and this ushered in what was commonly known as 'the hungry 30s'. While this economic dearth might have created physical hunger among Belfast's population, it did not lessen their spiritual appetite which still prevailed throughout those years. On the outskirts of East Belfast the British government built the new iconic edifice known as Stormont which was opened in 1932 to accommodate the recently created Northern Ireland Parliament. At the same time, the Lord was building His church through the work and witness of His servants in West Belfast.

Jack Johnston's constant emphasis on evangelism led to many fruitful evangelistic campaigns that were regularly conducted at the Welcome Hall during the 1930s. God blessed these evangelistic campaigns and because of their success the work at the Hall continued to grow.

* * * * *

In 1932 Julius Lipton, a converted Jew from the United States, came to the Welcome Hall for a month of special evangelistic meetings. After three weeks of Gospel mission seventy souls were saved. This was the beginning of another wave of spiritual awakening in the district.

* * * * *

Another American, Dr George Guest Williams, a noted expository preacher and Bible teacher from the Christian and Missionary Alliance, came to the Welcome in 1934 for a special series of meetings. As a consequence of his ministry a joint Bible class for men and women was started at the Hall. The blessings which followed these meetings were the early rains and a foretaste of better things to come.

* * * * *

Even greater blessings were experienced in 1935 when the evangelist Mr Fred Brown, came to Belfast. Those who attended the meetings said that God broke through in a mighty way and Fred Brown's visit has often been described as the best and most powerful evangelistic mission the Welcome Hall ever experienced.

Fred Brown was born in Birmingham, Alabama, but later made his home in Chattanooga, Tennessee. He was converted at an old-fashioned Presbyterian meeting where he heard a message on Hell. Although he was only seven years old at the time of his conversion Fred explained his experience of salvation in a very graphic way, "Hell was so real I could smell the fumes from the pit and hear the screams of the dying; I could see myself and the worm and the fire of hell was not quenched."

Prior to entering college Fred Brown worked on the United States' railroads. The Rev Harold Brown of Lurgan Presbyterian

Church introduced Fred to Jack Johnston who subsequently arranged for him to come to the Welcome for a period of special meetings.

From the moment Fred Brown arrived on the Shankill, the seal of God was on his ministry. The church was packed to capacity for every single meeting. After all the seats were occupied, people resorted to sitting on the windowsills while the rest of the overflow crowd thronged outside the door. Jimmy Johnston, a zealous member of the Welcome Hall, was the soloist for the meetings and on a few occasions he even preached.

Jim Neill, a former elder at the Welcome, recalled those great days of blessing during Fred Brown's visit:

Those were times of heaven on earth. Hundreds were saved during that mission and are still going on today. Fred had great ability to paint word pictures to the extent that when he spoke of Peter stepping out of the boat to go to Jesus you could almost sense the lap of the water against the boat.

God moved in with great power and blessing, and souls were saved every night. On some nights the counsellors remained right through until midnight leading people to faith in Jesus Christ. There was a great air of expectancy among the people, and many were praying for the salvation of their family members and neighbours.

* * * * *

For many years Jack and Elizabeth Johnston had been praying for Jack Morton. Although he came out for the Lord during those meetings, Jack had great difficulty in securing the assurance of his salvation. There was great rejoicing late one night when they received the news that Jack had come right through for the Lord. After that Jack Morton became one of the pastor's right hand men in the Welcome Hall. For the rest of his life Jack remained a faithful member of the Welcome and was always a stalwart during times of difficulty and a steadying influence in every crisis that the pastor and people passed through.

Jack Johnston's mission at the Welcome had always been to rescue the perishing and care for the dying. During the years of his ministry there were many other notable conversions, each one a miracle of God's grace and a monument to His mercy. Jack's aim was not only to lead people to faith in Jesus Christ, but also to nurture and help them grow to Christian maturity and useful service for the Lord.

* * * * *

Bill Black was also converted in those halcyon days of rich blessings. Like many other unconverted men from the neighbourhood, Bill spent most of his evenings at one of the many pubs on the Shankill Road. While still a young man Bill became enslaved to the liquor bottle and was soon indulging in the evils that often accompany this addiction. Alcohol blocked his mind and was destroying his body.

Although jobs were difficult at that time Bill was relieved to find some casual employment at Wilton's Funeral Undertakers. One day when Wilton's needed extra pallbearers Bill was asked to fill the role. For the solemn occasion he had to wear a long black coat and a top hat to assist at a funeral at a particular home. After the bereaved family said their tearful farewells to their deceased loved one, Bill stepped forward to put the lid on the coffin. As he did so he was startled to see his own name engraved on the plaque on the coffin lid. Although he said nothing the sight of his name hit him like a bolt of lightning and sent a shiver down his spine.

Even with this sobering experience Bill tried to resist God's voice speaking to him about preparing for eternity. However, before midnight of that same day, although intoxicated with drink, Bill staggered into a home in Ottawa Street where an ill lady quoted John 3:16 and confronted Bill with his need of Jesus Christ. That night Bill Black could withstand the Saviour no longer. He finally fell to his knees and called upon God salvation.

Although Bill's life was completely transformed by the power of God, he did encounter one particular moment of weakness after his conversion. He had always kept a five-glass bottle of spirits in a narrow wall recess in the shop where he worked. One day Bill decided to have a single drink from the bottle. Very carefully he tried to lift the bottle out of the recess, but as he did so he grazed the bottle against the stone on the corner of the recess. Just as if a glazier had purposely cut the bottle, the bottom fell out of it and the contents spilled over the floor. Bill was sure that God was the Glazier who had destroyed the bottle and delivered him from the evils of liquor. After that Bill Black never did touch another drop of alcohol.

Soon after his conversion Bill was accepted as a student at the Faith Mission Training Home in Edinburgh. He wanted to use his life in Christian service. It was at Edinburgh he met Tilly, his future wife. Tilly, who was from a small farm near Rasharkin, County Antrim, was also in training at the Faith Mission College.

When Bill and Tilly were married, instead of the bride wearing a wedding gown she wore her Faith Mission uniform complete with her black stockings and the traditional Faith Mission bonnet with its trimmings. Once married they were designated to work with the Faith Mission in Dunfermline and the Highlands where they successfully served the Lord in evangelistic ministry. Bill eventually became a District Superintendent for the Faith Mission in the Highlands. After several years in Scotland Bill and Tilly were transferred to Ballymena where they headed up the Faith Mission's operations in that area of county Antrim until Bill passed away.

* * * * *

In 1935 a Gospel quintet of black musicians from Cleveland, Ohio, USA, arrived at the Welcome Hall for another series of special meetings. The people were amazed to find out that back in the USA this quintet had attracted large congregations wherever they went, yet they were humble enough to come and serve the Lord for a few weeks at the Welcome Hall in Cambrai Street. The group›s leader, Brother Lacey, and his wife, stood facing one another on the platform and sang many Gospel songs to the glory of God. One catchy song the people enjoyed was 'The Grumbler's Song'. They brought great gladness to the people who at times were overwhelmed with the joy of the Lord and were greatly blessed as they listened to these gifted singers blend their voices in great harmony to sing the Gospel songs.

* * * * *

As a young man Jimmy Trew left Ligoniel in Belfast and immigrated to the United States. While there he was converted to Jesus Christ, and afterwards he entered into the Christian ministry. Jimmy's wife, an American, had exceptional skills with many different musical instruments and deftly played them at the meetings. During a return visit to Northern Ireland in 1936

Jimmy conducted special meetings at the Welcome Hall at which he preached and Mrs Trew enthralled those who attended by playing the xylophone.

* * * * *

Fred Brown made a return visit to the Welcome Hall in 1937, but on this occasion his new bride accompanied him. She also was a very gifted musician and prior to marrying Fred she had conducted a very popular radio programme every morning at seven o'clock. During Fred's second visit to the Welcome God again blessed his ministry and many souls were saved.

* * * * *

The growing congregation at the Welcome Hall was greatly blessed again in 1939 when the Rev Gnania Jos from India paid a visit to Belfast. Prior to his conversion Gnania had been a devout disciple of the great Gandhi, and toured India with his famous mentor. For years Gnania had been engaged in propagating Ghandi's message until one day he came to know Jesus Christ as Saviour. His dramatic conversion completely changed the direction of his life. Rev Gnania Jos's visit to the Welcome Hall was accompanied with great blessings. Those present said it was a real revival, for the Hall was packed every night with many people standing outside the doors and windows trying to see and hear what was going on inside.

Before the Rev Jos preached one evening he announced the well-known hymn, "*Who is on the Lord's side? Who will serve the King?*" The service was suddenly interrupted in the middle of the hymn when a very tall man stood up and said, "I will be on the Lord's side I will serve the King."

No sooner had he spoken than many others all over the congregation stood to their feet and publicly voiced their allegiance to God. The Holy Spirit swept through the congregation that night and the preaching was set aside so that counsellors could assist those who wanted to get right with God. All over the church people were crying out for forgiveness and asking God for a deeper experience in sanctification. Revival fires had been ignited during those days of Gnania Jos's visit and as a result many people had dealings with God.

* * * * *

Throughout the decade before World War II Mr Johnston continued to organise evangelistic missions at the Welcome Hall. He had a passion to win the lost for Christ, and God honoured his faithful ministry in the salvation of many souls.

In all this work Mr Johnston was fully supported by the faithful band of spiritual Welcome Hall members around him. Charlie Hamil, who was Pastor Johnston's right hand man, was always available to help in any way possible. Jim White Sr and Sam Morrow worked behind the scenes to maintain the hall in good condition. The growth of the Sunday School made it necessary to appoint an able superintendent, and Sam Art, a university graduate, fitted that role perfectly.

The flame of revival that had motivated Jack and Elizabeth Johnston burned all the more brightly because of the fine team of helpers the Lord had given to them.

CHAPTER 11

Blessings During the Blitz

The British government declared war on Germany in September 1939 after Nazi troops invaded Poland. Thousands of young men and women from Northern Ireland joined the services and marched, flew or sailed off to the battle front in a war that would last for more than five years. Many of them remained in uniform for the full duration of the conflict. Sadly, others, like the brave men of the First World War, paid the ultimate price and never returned home again.

At the start of the war it was thought that Belfast would be safe from any aerial attacks from the Germans as the city was simply too far away for Luftwaffe bombers to reach. However, that calculation was grossly misplaced. Belfast's shipyards, aircraft factories and engineering works were making too great a contribution to the British war effort for the German forces to ignore.

The peace in the city was shattered on the night of April 7th/8th 1941 when the Luftwaffe launched its first raid on the city with eight German planes testing Belfast's defences in an exploratory air raid on the city. (Five hundred Luftwaffe planes bombed Glasgow and Clyde shipyards on the same night). Facing minimal resistance in Belfast, the Germans dropped about eight hundred incendiary bombs on the dock area of the city. Thirteen people were killed that night and the houses of the heavily populated area were left in a heap of rubble.

The city was not really prepared for another German onslaught at midnight on 14th April 1941 when two hundred Luftwaffe bombers returned to inflict more appalling disaster on individuals and extensive destruction to property. More than nine hundred people died as a result of the aerial bombardment, and over one thousand five hundred citizens were injured.

It was also reckoned that besides the widespread destruction inflicted on the shipyards; factories, mills and churches, more than half of the houses in the city were damaged or destroyed. Burke Street, in the New Lodge area was wiped off the map with all its houses destroyed and most of the occupants killed. Percy Street on the lower Shankill Road suffered terribly when a German bomb had a direct hit on an air raid shelter where anxious neighbours had taken refuge. When the debris was cleared rescuers discovered that one bomb had killed thirty men, women and children from Percy Street.

All street lights were switched off at nightfall; it was obligatory for all residents to use dark blinds on their windows, and all vehicles had to use shaded lights. Despite these measures, they did not prevent the Germans from returning to the skies above Belfast. The wailing sound of sirens echoed across the city. Bright narrow beams from searchlights scanned the sky when another air raid took place on the night of Sunday 4 May 1941. The pounding sound of anti-aircraft fire was constant above the city. Sadly, another 150 people were killed that night.

The mills and factories around the Shankill Road and the Crumlin Road attracted the attention of the German pilots, and bombs were dropped on these places of popular employment. Consequently, as was the case in the Percy Street tragedy, many of the terraced houses in the tightly compacted Belfast streets were also destroyed. Whole families fled from their homes in desperate panic to find refuge in air-raid shelters or church halls while wardens and medics cared for the many casualties. Hundreds of people from the Shankill and Woodvale areas escaped out of the city to the Black Mountain at the head of the Ballygomartin Road where they spent many nights sleeping in the ditches.

Although bombs and incendiary devices seemed to be rained indiscriminately all over Belfast, business premises to the north and west of the city bore a greater part of the destruction. When incendiary bombs rained down on North Belfast the resulting fires engulfed buildings on the Crumlin Road, Antrim Road and York Road and lit up the sky.

Ruth Carson was raised in Leopold Street and she remembers as a teenager the whole family hiding in a small "coal hole" in her home on the night when incendiary bombs fell nearby on Disraeli Street and Ohio Street. Dozens of houses in these streets were reduced to heaps of smoldering rubble, and scores of neighbours were killed.

Some areas on the east of the city also experienced similar damage, but not comparable to the devastation inflicted on the north of the city. Industries, such as Ewart's Weaving Mill on the Crumlin Road, businesses, churches and houses suffered serious damage. The skies over the Crumlin Road glowed when an incendiary bomb made a direct hit on Crumlin Road Presbyterian Church. The aftermath was a veritable inferno on which local firemen gallantly doused water in a vain attempt to extinguish the leaping flames. On the following morning it was obvious that this former place of worship had been reduced to a heap of rubble. The terrace of houses on the adjoining Ewarts Row were also set alight with the incendiary bombs, and some of the residents had been incinerated in the blaze. It was a terrible and unforgettable night.

In the ensuing chaos and emergency the Welcome Hall, the scene of great blessing and revival during the years leading up to the war, was suddenly transformed into a temporary morgue. So great was the toll of victims of the blitz that provisional morgues sprung up all over Belfast. Besides the thousands who were left homeless, many people returned to their dwellings only to find them in a mess, the roof uncovered, doors blown off and windows smashed. In some places it was too dangerous to go home because of unexploded bombs and landmines lodged in the ground. Those were days of complete chaos.

Tilly Snoddon, a member at the Welcome Hall, told of one lady who on a night when people were being evacuated from their homes, said to an air-raid warden, "Hey mister, I need to go back to my house, for I have left my false teeth behind."

To this the stern warden replied, "Don't be daft lady. It's bombs they're dropping on us, not buns."

Mr and Mrs Johnston rallied the members of the Welcome to help as best they could with families on Cambrai Street and the surrounding neighbourhood. Because of the on-going dangers and threats of more air raids over Belfast whole households were evacuated out of the city to stay with families in more rural areas all over Northern Ireland. People remaining in the city were supplied with gas masks and periodic drills and tests on how and when to use them were carried out in all areas.

With young men gone to the war and families evacuated from the city, the attendance at most church services was greatly diminished. Nevertheless, Mr Johnston maintained a full programme of meetings through most of the war years. He was always adept at coining catchy phrases and using them at appropriate times. During the war years the general public was admonished to be vigilant about loose talk. The government posted placards all over the country, which declared, "Careless talk costs lives." Jack Johnston told the Welcome Hall people that this was a timely injunction for all talebearers. He went on to quote King David's lament over the death of King Saul, "Tell it not in Gath, publish it not in the streets of Askelon lest the daughters of the Philistines rejoice" (2 Samuel 1:20).

When the global conflict finally ended in 1945 with VE Day (Victory in Europe) in May and VJ Day (Victory in Japan) in August, there was great rejoicing all over the nation. Soon soldiers, sailors and airmen were returning home, some from active service and others from prisoner of war camps. Some soldiers and sailors were badly maimed from war wounds, and the others were grateful to have survived the terrible hostilities. Soon life in Belfast was able to return to a form of normality even though the nation was left impoverished and food and clothing were still rationed.

The austerity and impoverishment of that era probably made an important contribution in making people aware of their need of God and the Gospel in their lives. Mr Johnston and his friends continued to engage with the local community and minister to their needs. They invested time in making regular visits to meet families in their homes and were ready to help in whatever way possible. This social contact resulted in many people attending meetings at the Welcome Hall. Mr Johnston's labours were greatly rewarded when he was able to lead some of these people to trust Jesus Christ as Saviour. The blessings continued to be showered on the Lord's work at the Welcome Hall.

Evangelism was still the great emphasis of Pastor Johnston's ministry and he often used innovative ways to reach the local community. Concerned for those who did not attend any Gospel meetings the pastor decided to purchase an old tricycle that had been formerly used by the Post Office for parcel deliveries. He equipped the tricycle with a twelve-volt car battery to power a gramophone and an amplifier. With a team of workers from the Welcome he conducted more open-air meetings all over the Shankill area. Mr Johnston made sure the old tricycle was recycled to find a new life that made better deliveries.

While on duty on the Shankill Road, RUC officer, Sergeant Graham, could not fail to hear the personal testimonies and Gospel witness of the Welcome's open-air team. God spoke to the sergeant that night as he was crossing the road. Before the end of the evening Sergeant Graham trusted Jesus Christ as Saviour. This law enforcer became a recipient of God's amazing grace.

On the other side of the law was a man who was known to be a kleptomaniac with a strange addiction to stealing alarm clocks. When he was finally caught red handed the police discovered alarm clocks hidden in every part of his house. Needless to say he got time--he was sentenced to several months in Crumlin Road Prison; however, after this man had paid his debt to society he heard the Gospel, trusted Christ as Saviour and his life was transformed. The same man became a very active worker at the Welcome Hall and was greatly used in steering young people away from crime and bad company and guiding them into the paths of righteousness. He was also a great encourager to outgoing missionaries from the Welcome Hall and faithfully supported them while they were on their fields of service.

Jessie McConnell remembers that during those war years her mum, Sadie Crangle, and Granny Thompson took her by the hand for the short walk from her home to attend Sunday School at The Welcome. Jack Morton was the superintendent of school which was made up of scores of infant and teenage boys and girls who learned the Scriptures weekly. Jessie was only six years old when she accepted the Lord Jesus as her Saviour at The Welcome on 7th October 1946. That vital step, taken at such a tender age, determined the course of her whole life.

It was in that same year, 1946, that Jessie's dad, Solomon Crangle, who had recently been demobbed from the Royal Air Force, also trusted Jesus Christ as Saviour. His conversion came about as a result of the open-air meetings conducted nearby at Woodvale Park. These conversions were an answer to Granny Thompson's and Jessie's mother's prayers. They had not only prayed for Solomon's safety during the war, but also for the salvation of their family.

Subsequently, Mr and Mrs Johnston were glad to see the whole Crangle family become part of the family fellowship at The Welcome for years to come.

DR. GEORGE GUEST WILLIAMS

Bible Teacher : Evangelist,
Philadelphia, U.S.A.
Member Christian and Missionary Alliance,
Founded by A. B. Simpson, D.D., New York.

WILL (D.V.) CONDUCT

A GOSPEL CAMPAIGN

in the

Welcome Hall, Cambrai Street

(Off Shankill Road),

Commencing on Lord's Day,

2nd September, 1934.

Hours of Meeting—
Lord's Day, 11-30, 3-45, 7-30.
Week-nights. 8 o'c

Soloists—Messrs. W. G. Hill and R M'Cready
Ravenhill Male Quartette and others will take part.

Don't miss hearing this wonderful Bible Teacher and Evangelist.

A Hearty Welcome awaits you.

Seats Free.   Hymn Books provided.

" And the Spirit and the Bride say come, and whosoever will may come.'
Rev.. 22–17.

N.B.—Our Bible Class for men and women reopens for
the Winter Session on Lord's Day Afternoon, Sept. 2nd,
3-45 o'clock.   Speaker-Dr. Williams,

CHAPTER 12

Aftermath of the War

The people of Northern Ireland survived the austerity of the 1930s, the terrible atrocities of World War II and the continuing threat of civil strife, but in the late 1940s they faced a new challenge of adjusting to life in the post-war United Kingdom. There was very little affluence in Northern Ireland. Food, furniture and clothing continued to be rationed until the early 1950s. In the immediate years after the war most homes still did not have electricity, and their furnishings were quite basic.

The Welcome Hall structure reflected the plainness of those times. Amy Carmichael had passed away in 1951 when she was eighty-three years old. There is no doubt that she had left behind a remarkable legacy which all began with her work at the Welcome Hall. However, in the same year in which Amy died the original corrugated tin tabernacle that she had purchased almost sixty years earlier had changed very little. It was not very pretentious. The old hall was still heated by two coal burning potbelly stoves placed on either side of the hall. These glowed when they were full ablaze, but sometimes filled the hall with smoke when they were being lit. The plain wooden forms were not designed for comfortable seating during long sermons. The rafters still had large hooks to carry the weight of swings that were used by the mill girls in Amy's time at the Welcome Hall. Very little had changed at the Welcome during the first half of the twentieth century. Several times each year Pastor

Johnston organised a work party to scrub the wooden floors and clean the old hall. After the work was finished the pastor bought fish and chips for all the workers.

Jack Johnston passed through his own experience of sorrow and had to adjust to a new phase in his life when Mrs Johnston passed away on 16th January 1948. Elizabeth Johnston had been Jack's faithful helpmate, his constant companion, the provider of their material needs and a frequent encourager in his work at the Welcome Hall. She was greatly missed not only by Pastor Johnston, but by all who knew her at the Welcome.

At a meeting of the trustees of the Welcome Hall in March 1948 they recorded a minute regretting Mrs Johnston's death:

The Chairman (Mr W S Mitchell) referred to the death of Mrs Johnston, wife of the Superintendent, and the great loss to the work at the Welcome Hall where she had so faithfully assisted her husband over a long period of years. A resolution of sympathy was passed to Mr Johnston by the meeting standing in silence.

The Chairman was requested to write to Mr Johnston on behalf of the Trustees conveying an expression of their sympathy in the great loss he had sustained.

Mrs Brownrigg reported that she had an interview with Mr Johnston, and the Trustees would be glad to hear that Mr Johnston was prepared to carry on the work as heretofore and at the next meeting of the Trustees Mr Johnston be requested to attend and give a report about the work going on at the Welcome Hall.

In memory of Mrs Johnston and with gratitude for that work, some kind friends purchased and donated a Communion Table and two chairs for the use of the Welcome Hall. The trustees graciously accepted this kind gesture. Jack Johnston had established a communion service at the Hall in the early 1930's, but they never had a proper Communion Table. Having a communion service became a matter of debate among the trustees some of whom thought that the work of the Welcome Hall was that of a mission and not a church. Mr Johnston's leadership and gentle persuasion eventually prevailed.

After Elizabeth's passing Pastor Johnston returned to live in Ballinderry for a short while. In her book, *Kohila: the Shaping of an Indian Nurse*, Amy Carmichael wrote, "The word comfort is from two Latin words meaning "with" and "strong" – He is with us to make us strong. Comfort is not soft, weakening commiseration; it is true, strengthening love." Jack Johnston found that comfort in the Lord; he also found strength to continue on in the work God had called him to. At first he commuted back and forth between Ballinderry and the Welcome Hall in all sorts of weather on a Vespa Scooter. This arrangement was not very satisfactory either for the pastor or for his pastoral work at the Welcome. Bobby and Tilly Snoddon were quick to recognise this and kindly extended an invitation to the pastor to stay at their home any weekend he needed.

Pastor Johnston gladly accepted their kind invitation. He travelled to Cambrai Street every Saturday and stayed with Bobby and Tilly until the following Wednesday. This arrangement proved to be a great help to the pastor and a blessing to the Snoddons. Jack loved the hospitality, friendship and fellowship at Bobby and Tilly's home. The three of them were people of like mind and equally dedicated to the Lord's work at the Welcome Hall.

Of course, there were other dedicated members at the Welcome. The building might not have been much to look at, but Pastor Johnston's ministry had produced some great saints who gave their time and substance to maintain the work. The streets of heaven are filled with stories of redeemed sinners who served their Lord on earth.

* * * * *

Billy Creighton was a teacher in the Welcome Sunday School when he heard God's call to full-time missionary service. Billy joined the Baptist Missions and for twenty-three years he served the Lord as a pioneer missionary until the Lord called him home to higher service.

* * * * *

After his conversion Samuel Clemence spent most of his early Christian years at the Welcome. He went from the Welcome to train for the Methodist ministry. Samuel served the Lord in various Methodist churches in Ireland until his retirement.

* * * * *

Sam Calderwood's early Christian life began at the Welcome Hall. From there he went on to become a Baptist pastor. Likewise, Alfie Williamson also was a part of the fellowship at the Welcome Hall before going on to the Presbyterian ministry. Jim White went further afield. After his early days in the Welcome Jim left Northern Ireland and became a pastor in the United States of America. There is no doubt that the influence and impact of Pastor Johnston's ministry at the Welcome was felt around the world.

Jim Neil, who held a very responsible position at the Belfast Newsletter, was an elder at the Welcome Hall. Besides his much appreciated spiritual maturity and insightful wisdom, Jim was a very good singer and organised a musical group known as "The Celestial Singers". Although they were in great demand to use their musical gift in other churches they refused to neglect their work at the Welcome. No doubt Pastor Johnston made sure that his singers gave priority to the work at the Hall. He had no hesitation in telling his members what was expected of them.

* * * * *

Like Jim Grainger had done years earlier, Bobby Milliken also went to the Belgian Congo with the WEC. He and his wife Ivy spent over thirty years serving the Lord in the primeval African forests with a primitive tribe at Pamia.

Norman Grubb, son-in-law of the founder of the WEC, CT Studd, made mention of Bobby's involvement in the conversion of a godless man in his book, *A Mighty Word of the Spirit*:

Our last bush conference was not in the bush, but in an unusual place, a trading centre, at Bambisa. I had not before seen a church and school right among the shops, with a Portuguese trader living opposite, for these trading centres are usually sinks of iniquity. This one was no exception, till the leading African shop man was saved. What a character! He was a great strapping fellow, godless and fearless. Once a white official had come with twelve police to give him a whipping for his lawless behaviour, but he drew a knife and said to the official, 'Come and give it me yourself, and if you do, you will get this in your bowels.'

He got no thrashing! What a change now! 'I had,' he said, 'the heart of a beast.' But, though an evil-living man with a wife and seven concubines, he wanted children and had none. One day he was given a New Testament. He could not read, but had heard God answers prayer, so he opened the book and asked for children. That night in a dream, a man stood by him and said, 'You are heard. You will have two children, a girl and a boy, and after that many children.' And so it came to pass. The girl and boy were born, and he began to seek God in earnest.

When Bobby Milliken came that way, he spoke to him and said, "I must have God."

'Then you must give up your concubines.' Bobby told him.

'Certainly,' he said immediately, 'but I must have God.'

'And the blood came,' he later said, 'and killed things for me. Adultery, shame, wine, all went. Can anything else do that? Only the Blood of Jesus.'

When he told us this, we were in the church with about one hundred believers, and he looked round on them and said, "And here are my many children."

Owing to the unsettled conditions in Congo following the Zimba uprising in 1964, Bobby and his wife Ivy left Africa and went to pioneer a work in Northern France. While there he established the Miners Mission in France. After seventeen years of mission work in France Bobby and Ivy retired to England where they carried on a similar evangelistic work among the coal miners.

* * * * *

While the Welcome sent a number of missionaries to Africa Mr Johnston and his friends were greatly honoured to receive a visit from a very distinguished African guest in 1951. Prince Makonnen, the son of the Emperor Haile Selassie I of Ethiopia, paid a visit to Amy's modest tin tabernacle. Prince Makonnen was a very keen Christian, and it was not below his dignity to be associated with the humble surroundings at the Welcome.

God blessed the Prince when he gave his testimony that night. At the end of the service he spoke a group of young men and virtually obliged them to go to the enquiry room to seek the Lord. One of those young men really did come through for God that night. His name was Roy Kernaghan who in the following years would make a big contribution to the work at the Welcome Hall.

Roy related how God changed his life that night:

On 22nd August 1951 I attended the Wednesday night Gospel service in the Welcome Mission Hall, now the Welcome Evangelical Church. The visiting speaker was the grandson of the Emperor of Ethiopia, Haili Selassie. The singer that night was Alma McArthur who later married Bobby McAllister. Bob and Alma were missionaries fo considerable renown with UFM in the Belgian Congo.

At the close of the meeting the preacher asked all the Christians to stand and for the unconverted to remain seated. Being one of the unconverted I remained in my seat. The preacher then came round the hall appealing to those who were seated to trust Christ as Saviour. My companion, John Daly, arose immediately and went into the inquiry room. Soon afterwards I followed him when the preacher came by and appealed to me. I was led to saving faith in Jesus Christ that night. I did not have any great emotional feeling nor did I see any flash of lightening. That night I received a great Saviour, a great salvation and since then I have known great peace in my heart and am living with a great prospect.

Sixty-two years have passed since that August night in 1951. I am now an eighty-two years old. Through all these years Christ has been my strength in weakness, my comfort in sorrow and my peace in the storms of life. Praise God for Him. AMEN.

The post-war austerity on the Shankill was greatly compensated for by a sense of community, neighbours helping neighbours and many of them meeting each other at the Welcome Hall.

Welcome Hall Outing 1952

CHAPTER 13

The Young Brothers

God's work often involves passing the baton from one generation to another. Mr Johnston had been serving the Lord at the Welcome Hall for more than twenty years when a young man started to attend the meetings in 1948. Eddie Young's arrival at the Welcome was to make a big impact on his own life, on the lives of countless scores of people at home and abroad and on the future of the work at the Welcome Hall.

Eddie grew up in a happy home in Farringdon Gardens in Ardoyne even though his father, a soldier in the British Army, was absent during the war years. He always looked up to his older brother Harry and enjoyed the company and fun of his three sisters, May, his older sister, and his two younger sisters, Myrtle and Betty.

Mrs Young and her five children had great joy to see the end of World War II, for not only was her husband home from the army and back to life on civic street, but the five children had a father to look up to and help guide them through lives.

Although all the Young children attended Everton School on the nearby Crumlin Road, they did seek other pursuits after school hours. While other boys played football or hung around the street corners Harry Young enlisted as a recruit in the Army Cadet Force. He had undoubtedly been influenced to make this decision because his dad had been a soldier. Marching drills and physical training exercises at the weekend Cadet Force camps kept Harry busy and physically fit. The development of his physical vigour greatly appealed to Harry, for he was a member of the Short and Harland Amateur Boxing Club at Huss Street in the heart of the Shankill, but when his boxing career developed he moved to another boxing club in Castle Lane, near to the city centre.

When the Army Cadet officers learned of Harry's considerable talents in the boxing ring they entered him for inter-army competitions. He quickly rose through the ranks, and while he was still in his mid-teens Harry won the Northern Ireland Pre-service Boxing Championship as a featherweight. Soon he was fighting in the British National Championships. By the time he reached nineteen years old Harry had become an acclaimed international boxer.

On one occasion he was boxing an opponent much bigger than himself. No one intimidated Harry. He knocked his rival out of the ring three times before the fight was finally stopped in Harry's favour.

Mr Young took great interest and pride in Harry's prowess, development and success in the boxing ring. Younger brother Eddie was also so greatly impressed by Harry's accomplishments as a boxer that he also decided to join the Short and Harland Amateur Boxing Club.

During his training programme at the club Eddie's skills also became obvious to his trainers. The club's coaches successfully guided their young prodigy through various bouts in the amateur lightweight divisions. Eddie was soon boxing in the Amateur Boxing Association Lightweight Ulster Championship.

Eddie fought a series of eliminating bouts at various clubs all over Belfast; Bell's Club, the Long Bar Club, the Whiterock Club and his own club, Short and Harland Amateur Boxing Club. On one occasion he even had to fight two bouts in one night. Eddie won many of these fights by overwhelming decisions, and one poor opponent had to be taken to hospital after a pounding from Eddie. He finally qualified to fight in the final at Belfast's favourite boxing venue, the Ulster Hall.

Although he was beaten in that Ulster Hall final Eddie did qualify to box for the All Ireland Amateur Lightweight Boxing Championships in Dublin. He was really looking forward to the challenge and spent every possible moment training and preparing for this prestigious event. However, something happened on the way home from the boxing club one day that arrested Eddie's progress as a boxer and changed the course of his life.

Eddie was nearing his Ardoyne home that summer evening, June 1948, when he came upon an open-air meeting on a street corner. Mr Forbes, the missionary at the nearby Belfast City Mission, was preaching the Gospel in the hope that passers-by and local residents might listen to the good news about Jesus Christ. Instead of passing by Eddie stopped to listen to the open-air preacher for a few minutes. Even though he did not hang around for very long, Eddie heard sufficient that evening from the ardent evangelist to trouble his conscience.

As he made his way home he began to turn over in his mind the Gospel truths he had heard: he was a sinner and Jesus Christ came into the world to save sinners. Although he knew that pardon, peace and salvation were gifts to receive, he was also aware that denying Christ and dying without Christ would result in being lost in hell for all eternity. These vital truths troubled the young teenager even after he arrived home. He tried to escape from them in his mind, but found himself recalling the Gospel truths his former teacher at Everton School, Mr McCullough, had instilled in him.

Mr McCullough was a member of the Oldpark Brethren Assembly and besides being a very good school teacher, he also made good use of his position to teach the Gospel to his students every morning at the school assembly or in the classroom. What Eddie had learned at those morning talks never left him and now they perturbed him as he tried to dispense them from his uneasy mind and troubled soul.

In his attempt to dismiss the mounting conviction in his heart Eddie tried to rationalise the reasons why he could not become a Christian: *What would people say? What would I do about the boxing? How am I going to tell people that I am a Christian? What will the members of the band think?*

In vain Eddie tried to raise these objections and coax himself out of facing up to his great spiritual need. He finally broke down and sank to his knees at the side of his bed. He confessed to God that he was a sinner and asked the Lord Jesus to come into his heart and be his Saviour. Once he had made that vital decision and had taken that important step a great sense of relief came over him. Eddie knew he had been converted, born again, and was now a Christian.

Of course, Eddie still had to face his family, his brother and sisters and then the sceptical public. At that time Eddie was working for McMullen & Mitchell, shop fitters, on the Holywood Road in East Belfast. As he made his way to work the next morning he tried to work out a strategy of how he would break the news to his workmates that he had become a Christian. Eddie knew that one of the apprentices was an Anglican churchgoer and felt that he would probably have the most sympathetic ear for the news of his conversion. How wrong he was. When Eddie told the young apprentice that he had become a Christian the previous night, the teenager reacted with great resentment and said, "Don't you be giving me any of this Gospel stuff. I have had enough of that."

Eddie was stunned. He unwittingly thought that everybody who attended church loved the Lord Jesus Christ. On that morning he learned that religiosity and Christianity are not synonymous or even compatible. However, news of Eddie's conversion soon seeped out among the other workers. At the midmorning tea-break one of them, Isaac, jokingly said to Eddie, "Come on and tell us your story Eddie."

It was just the opportunity Eddie needed. Prior to this all his work mates respected him for his boxing skills and success. Now they were flabbergasted as they listened to Eddie tell how he had accepted Jesus Christ as Saviour.

One day while Eddie was working as an apprentice joiner alongside Cecil, a tough tradesman at the same shop-fitting establishment, Cecil let fly a few unsavoury expletives. Eddie was not only taken aback at the joiner's foul language, but also a little fearful to speak up. He asked God to give him strength and then told Cecil that he was a Christian and did not like to hear those profanities.

Cecil looked Eddie in the eye and said, "Why didn't you tell me you were a Christian? If you had told me I would have respected that and tried not to curse." Thereafter, Cecil, although he was looked on as a rough and tough man, always respected Eddie and avoided using bad language when he was in Eddie's presence.

Before his conversion Eddie was learning to play the chanter in a local bagpipe band. His aim was to eventually learn how to play the bagpipes. When he told the bandleaders that he had become a Christian they were quick to show him the door. They had no time for Christians and sent Eddie packing. That was the end of his chanter lessons and bagpipe career.

After his conversion Eddie realised he needed Christian company. It was at that time that his friendship with Andy Taggart, from Twadell Avenue had a great influence on him. Andy, like Eddie, was very much involved in his boxing career, and the two young men struck up a friendship at Short and Harland Amateur Boxing Club. Eddie was glad when he learned that Andy also was a Christian.

Andy was another boxing prodigy at the Short and Harland Amateur Boxing Club. He successfully fought at the flyweight division at the time of Eddie's conversion and was in training for and eventually won the Rose Bowl, a highly celebrated achievement at that time.

Not long after their conversion Andy suggested to Eddie that they should go down to the Welcome Hall on Sunday evening. When they got to "the wee mission hall", as Andy had called it, the two young men were immediately drawn by the warm welcome, the enthusiastic singing and Bible preaching.

Eddie had found his spiritual home and very soon the Welcome Hall was his regular place of worship.

CHAPTER 14

The Acceptable Year of the Lord

The Welcome Hall not only became Eddie Young's spiritual home, very soon he was becoming more and more involved in the work at the Hall. Mr Johnston was quick to see the potential in this young man and therefore, encouraged him to teach a group of boys at the Sunday Bible Class. Even though Eddie was a little apprehensive about his ability to teach the Scriptures he decided to accept the challenge. This responsibility to teach at the weekly Bible Class was the incentive Eddie needed to help him study the Word of God even more.

Another aspect of the work at the Welcome Hall that impressed Eddie Young was the WEC Prayer Battery at the home of Bobby and Tilly Snoddon at 6 Olive Street. Every week forty young people met at Bobby and Tilley's home to pray for WEC missionaries all over the world. Periodically visiting missionaries came to speak at this prayer meeting, and on other weeks Bobby read out news from missionaries who had visited the meeting on former occasions. Eddie soon became familiar with the names of these missionaries, got to know some of them and prayed for them.

At the same time, Eddie was keen to invite his brother Harry to the meetings at the Welcome. Harry was continuing to pursue his career as a boxer and was riding life on the crest of the wave, at least, so he thought. Sadly, Harry had become an addicted gambler.

His addiction was so great that at times he went so far as to pawn his clothes in exchange for a few pounds to put another bet on the dogs. When he failed to get a return on that bet, Harry went so far as to even take Eddie's clothes to the pawnshop to lay his hands on more money for a bet at the bookies.

Harry was always the centre of attention and became identified with a gang of young men from Ardoyne. His dress code always reflected the trends of young people at that time, wearing narrow 'drainpipe' trousers and bright yellow colours.

Notwithstanding Harry's addiction and lifestyle, Eddie always had great respect for his older brother and enjoyed a good relationship with him. For that reason he invited Harry to attend the Sunday evening evangelistic meeting at the Welcome Hall. Eddie was a little surprised, but very glad that Harry accepted his invitation. Now he set about earnestly praying that the Lord would save his older brother.

Harry's trendy appearance made him quite conspicuous and a little bit uneasy when he sat down beside the more conservatively dressed churchgoers at the Welcome. He became more restless as he listened to the singing and the preaching. He kept looking at his watch and hoping that the meeting would soon be over. Immediately after Mr Johnston finished his final prayer Harry left the building in quite a hurry. It seemed that Eddie's first attempt to win his brother for Christ had been frustrated, for Harry vowed to him that he would never be back to a meeting at the Welcome Hall.

Eddie said nothing more to Harry about the meeting or the Gospel during the next week, but he did continue to pray that God would speak to him. Providentially, by the end of that week Harry was virtually penniless because of another ill-fated wager he had placed on a dog which had failed to win the race. With no money in his pocket Harry had nowhere else to go on Sunday night. In spite of what he had avowed earlier, Harry asked Eddie if he was going back to the Welcome Hall that night. Eddie could hardly believe it when his brother volunteered to go back to the meeting just one week after declaring that he would never be back.

God answered Eddie's prayers, for on that Sunday night in 1949 Harry Young trusted Jesus Christ as personal Saviour. God totally transformed his life. Harry turned his back on the "Teddy Boy" gang, his addiction to gambling and the lure of fame in a promising boxing career. He joined the ranks of other Christian young people at the Welcome Hall where he redirected all the energies into serving his Lord.

Initially, Eddie's involvement in the work at the Welcome did not prohibit him from still pursuing his boxing ambitions. However, that was to change in a most unexpected way. Although he had been converted Eddie was a little hesitant to tell his training team at the Short & Harland Club that he was a Christian. He knew it was something he should do and would have to do, but in his heart and mind he wrestled with how he was going to confess Christ to them. While Eddie was turning these things over in his mind, the Scriptures seemed to come to him, "Man looks on the outward appearance, but God looks on the heart." It was then that Eddie realised that this was his problem; he had been looking at the boxing fraternity and thought they were tough people. For that reason he had been fearful of speaking to them about Christianity and his conversion.

One night after Eddie had completed a sparring session, his trainer, William, was rubbing him down. As he did so William peppered his language with some blasphemous and profane words. Eddie was disturbed to hear these casual profanities and mustered up the courage to ask the trainer not to swear as he had recently become a Christian.

The boxing trainer was taken aback at Eddie's news. "A Christian?" he asked. "If you are a Christian what are you doing here? This is no place for a Christian. Look at that fellow whose face you smashed up and split his lip. How could you beat the head of a fellow like that until his blood is flowing and then try to tell him that God loves him? There is no way that can be. This is certainly no place for you son."

At first Eddie was taken aback at the trainer's rebuke. He had enjoyed the training and the boxing. However, on the way home that night he realised that the trainer's reprimand was God's way of showing him that boxing was not compatible with being a Christian. By the time he arrived at his Farringdon Gardens' home he had decided not to go back to the boxing club. That night Eddie told his dad that he was packing in the boxing. His father could not believe it. "But you are in for the All Ireland Championships Eddie. Why give it up now?"

"No dad, I've become a Christian, and I don't want to box anymore." His mind was made up. Eddie gave his boxing gloves, his boots and all his gear to another young man who was training to be a boxer. From that time onwards Eddie's passion for the exchange of physical blows in the ring was exchanged for a more important struggle, a life-long conflict against the powers of darkness.

Not long after Eddie started to attend the Welcome Hall, Sadie Cosby, a teenage girl from a Christian home in Cambrai Street, also arrived at the Welcome. At that stage neither Eddie Young nor Sadie Cosby knew that God would bind them together in marriage, nor could they have envisaged all that God had for them in the future.

Two years prior to her arrival at the Welcome Hall, Sadie's godly parents were delighted when their fifteen year-old daughter trusted the Lord Jesus Christ as her Saviour. Sadie was converted through the ministry of the evangelist James Armstrong, who was conducting an evangelistic mission at the nearby Keswick Street Mission Hall.

For a short while after her conversion Sadie continued to attend the Keswick Street Hall where she developed an interest in missionaries and missions. Because of her interest in missions and missionaries a friend invited Sadie to the W.E.C. Prayer Battery at Bobby and Tilley Snoddon's house in Olive Street. At that meeting Sadie was even more challenged when she met forty other young people who had all gathered to pray for WEC missionaries.

Sadie soon made friends with the other young people at the Snoddon's home and as a result she began to attend the Welcome Hall. In the course of attending the Welcome Hall Sadie Cosby and Eddie Young got to know each other, and before long romance was blossoming between them. However, it was not only romance that drew Eddie and Sadie together. Through those WEC prayer meetings both of them heard God's call for foreign missionary service.

David and Margaret Barron from Belfast, who were WEC missionaries in Senegal and the Gambia, were invited to speak at the Snoddon's weekly prayer meeting one evening. On that night they shared their burden for the souls of Senegal and Western Africa with the assembled group of young people. Eddie Young listened intently to the two missionaries. He was so challenged by the great spiritual needs in Africa and the dedication of this Irish couple to the point of feeling constrained to offer himself for missionary service. On that very night when the young people knelt to pray Eddie yielded his will to God and silently, but sincerely, he volunteered to go where God might lead him.

Following this surrender to the Lord for Christian service, Eddie decided to speak to Mr Johnston about the matter, hoping and expecting that the good pastor would encourage him to step out into Christian work that very year. On the contrary, Eddie was surprised when the wise pastor restrained the young man's eagerness to apply for missionary training immediately. He counselled Eddie to continue as a Bible Class teacher at the Welcome Hall for at least another year. This advice was probably prompted by the fact that Eddie was heavily involved with the leadership of the young people at the Hall, and Mr Johnston needed him. Furthermore, this was good experience for Eddie.

Although Eddie was anxious to go to Bible College as soon as possible, he accepted the pastor's guidance. He had need of patience as he waited for the Lord to open the door in due course. Meanwhile, Eddie and Sadie kept on with their involvement in the work and outreach at the Welcome Hall under Pastor Johnston's leadership. Through the following months they also continued to be nurtured and challenged to a life of full surrender to the will of God. That constraint for missionary service wherever God might indicate never left their minds. The young couple talked about it and prayed about it while they waited for God's guidance.

At this time Eddie had a change of career. Instead of his apprenticeship with the shop-fitting firm he secured employment as a baker in the canteen of the Wolfhill Spinning Mill at Ligoneil. Eddie enjoyed learning the new skills and working in the kitchens. The only drawback for him was because he started work so early in the morning Eddie did not have time for much Bible reading before leaving home. He tried to remedy this by catching up with his Bible reading at his lunch hour.

One day during his lunch break he was sitting on top of a few sacks of flour reading his New Testament. As he read Luke 4 he came to the place where the Lord Jesus had entered the synagogue and opened the Scriptures at the book of Isaiah. Eddie was struck by what he read: "And when he had opened the book, he found the place where it was written, 'The Spirit of the Lord is upon me, because he hath anointed me to preach the Gospel to the poor; he hath sent me to heal the brokenhearted, to preach deliverance to the captives, and recovering of sight to the blind, to set at liberty them that are bruised, to preach the acceptable year of the Lord'" (Luke 4:17-19).

The words of verse 19 arrested Eddie, "...the acceptable year of the Lord." Mr Johnston had told him to wait for a year before thinking of going to a Bible College. His brother Harry had already given up his boxing career and had enrolled at All Nations Bible College in England to prepare for missionary service. As Eddie sat on the sacks of flour that day he was convinced that Luke 4:19 was God's word to him. For Eddie this was now "the acceptable year of the Lord." He felt it was time to make a move.

Eddie shared his experience with Sadie who was excited to hear of this development. He then announced to Mr Johnston that the Lord had called him to be a missionary and it was now time to apply for missionary training. Eddie knew that the WEC already had a flourishing Missionary Training College in Glasgow so he made application to enroll for the following autumn.

In 1951 Eddie left Belfast to study for two years at the Missionary Training College. During that time he was able to devote much more time to studying the Scriptures, learning theology and engaging in evangelistic tours across Scotland. He was also challenged when he listened to many missionaries speak of the great needs on their respective fields. Everyone had an appealing cause. However, Eddie could not forget how God spoke to him through David and Margaret Barron's report about the need for workers in Senegal on Africa's west coast.

Sadie had also planned to go to the same WEC Missionary Training College as Eddie, but she was only able to do so after he had completed his two-year course there. In those more restrictive times it was not permitted that couples should be in the Training College at the same time.

After Eddie completed his missionary training he applied to the WEC for the work in Senegal, and he was readily accepted. Following completion of the Candidate's Course at the WEC headquarters in London Eddie proceeded to France for language study.

In due course Eddie was sent out as a missionary from the Welcome Hall to Senegal in 1958. Meanwhile, Sadie followed through the same process as Eddie with her time at the Glasgow Missionary Training College and then her time at the Candidates' Course in the WEC headquarters in London. After she was accepted by the mission for the work in Senegal she went on to France to study French. Besides studying French, Sadie also worked as an au pair, which not only helped her language skills, but also helped to provide funds for her material needs. It was during her time in France that Sadie developed her life-long love for languages and literature.

Back in those days the WEC required engaged couples to be on the mission field for two years before they could be married. For that reason Sadie was always two years behind Eddie in her training and preparation for going to Africa. She finally arrived in Senegal in 1960. Soon afterwards they were married in the little evangelical church in Ziguinchor.

For the next twenty years Eddie and Sadie laboured extensively in different ministries in Senegal. Not only were they able to build a church in Ziguinchor, which is still functioning and flourishing, but also and more importantly, they were able to pour their lives into training African believers who became Christian workers and are still serving the Lord in Africa.

After twenty productive years of missionary service in Senegal circumstances changed and it became necessary for Eddie and Sadie to permanently return to Northern Ireland. When they left Africa they were unaware that the Lord had another challenge for them at the Welcome Hall.

Pastor Edward Young and his wife Sadie

CHAPTER 15

Serving the King

In Genesis 49 we read how the patriarch Jacob gathered his sons around him, and to each he imparted prophetic words regarding their future. His prophecies were a mixture of foretelling of blessings and blight that would follow his sons' pathway. To his favourite son, Joseph, who had suffered so much, Jacob said, "Joseph is a fruitful bough, even a fruitful bough by a well; whose branches run over the wall" (Genesis 49:22). The ancient patriarch was predicting that just as Joseph's prosperity and productive influence had saved Israel so his influence would also reach far beyond the bounds of Israel and be a blessing to the Gentile nations.

For many decades this same parallel has been duplicated in the work and witness of the Welcome Hall. Amy Carmichael, the founder of the mission, was the prototype of the principle that would be replicated in the hall for future generations. While the witness in the Shankill community was uppermost in the priority of Mr Johnston's ministry, the reach of that witness extended to the uttermost ends of the world. Through their missionaries the fruitful branches of the Welcome Hall's influence took blessings of Gospel grace to thousands of people around the world.

Harry Young's boxing ability gave him a measure of fame and popularity in his local community. However, when he became a Christian the lure of the crowds and the attraction of popularity and fame soon lost their lustre. Harry discovered that there were greater prizes to fight for, the prize that Paul spoke of in Philippians 3:13, 14: "This one thing I do, forgetting those things which are behind, and reaching forth unto those things which are before, I press toward the mark for the prize of the high calling of God in Christ Jesus." That heavenly prize became Harry's priority.

Like his brother Eddie, Harry was also richly nurtured and wisely guided by Pastor Johnston's faithful Bible teaching and guidance in his spiritual life. Indeed, the pastor confessed that he looked on Harry and Eddie Young as the Apostle Paul looked on Timothy and Titus; they were his true sons in the faith.

Through the pastor's constant call for full surrender to the will of God and his faithful Bible ministry Harry also felt the Lord was also leading him into fulltime Christian work. He always maintained that God had spoken to him in a most unusual and convoluted way. While he was reading in the prophecy of Isaiah he came on chapter 33:17: "Thine eyes shall see the king in his beauty: they shall behold the land that is very far off." On reading these words Harry asked God what 'far off land' the Lord had in mind for him.

Harry continued reading into the next chapter until he came to Isaiah 34:2; "For the indignation of the Lord is upon all nations..." This verse also struck him, but he continued to 36:11: " Then said Eliakim and Shebna and Joah unto Rabshakeh, 'Speak, I pray thee, unto thy servants in the Syrian language; for we understand it: and speak not to us in the Jews› language, in the ears of the people that are on the wall.'"

God dealings with each individual are personal and can only be interpreted on the basis of relationship. Through these extended readings Harry perceived the following; the "land afar off" was where God would have him go, "all nations" was the name of the college where he should train and "the Syrian language" would be the language he would have to learn. The first step in this plan for Harry was to enrol as a student for the two-year course at All Nations Bible College in 1953.

After he finished his studies Harry applied and was accepted by SIM International in the mid-1950s for their work in Syria, the land indicated in Isaiah 36:11. Initially Harry went to study Arabic at the mission's school for the blind. It was there that he met American missionary, Joann Eaton, who was already serving the Lord in that difficult country. Soon there was that irresistible chemistry of romance between Harry and Joann, and this resulted in them being married in 1958.

After learning Arabic Harry and Joann served the Lord with TEAM ministries for four years before moving to the United Arab Emirates (UAE) in 1962. It was while they were in UAE that they became members of WEC, and for the next ten years they served God in that country. Harry and Joann pioneered and established a medical work in the Gulf State and helped build up a New Testament Church in Dubai.

Due to complications with their son's health they had to move back to Birmingham, England, in the mid-1970s. Harry and Joann were able to put their Arabic to good use in the English Midlands over the next twenty-five years as they continued their Christian work among Muslims at colleges and universities. During this time Harry helped set up The Mission for Muslims Trust (TMFMT). Under the auspices of TMFMT he wrote many evangelistic leaflets and articles to be widely circulated in the Islamic world. Through this work Harry had the joy of leading many Muslims to faith in Jesus Christ. Harry's work was completed in 1998 when he died very suddenly and went to be with his Lord Whom he had served so well.

Many others Christian workers followed the challenging example left by the former great missionary pioneers who had gone to various mission fields from the Welcome Hall during Pastor Johnston's ministry. Billy Davidson went to serve God in South America; Alfred Williamson left the Welcome to go into the Presbyterian ministry and became the minister of the nearby Nelson Memorial Presbyterian Church; Jim White Jr., went to Cliff College in England before immigrating to the United States where he entered the Presbyterian ministry. Jim eventually became a chaplain to the U.S. Armed Forces.

Ella Scott was also sent from the Welcome to train at the WEC Missionary Training College in Glasgow. It was there that she met Brian Butcher. After Brian and Ella were married Brian became a Baptist pastor in Banbury, England. Ella Orr surrendered her life to serve God abroad, but she was prevented from going to a foreign mission field because of her hearing impairment.

John Adams, who was a founding member of the Woodvale Quartet, joined the Welcome Hall in the late 1940s. Besides having a very good baritone voice, John was a very gifted soul-winner. He later went to serve the Lord with the Dublin YMCA where he remained until his home call in 1998.

Philip Skelly served the Lord in the London City Mission for almost two years and then moved to help in a small Baptist Church on the east side of London.

Just as Joseph's productive life was a fruitful bough that blessed many nations, so also the Welcome Hall's fruitful branches reached far beyond their immediate boundaries to bless and benefit many other people through the Gospel.

CHAPTER 16

Betty and the Faith Mission

Betty Young, Harry and Eddie's sister and the youngest of the family, followed her older brothers into Christian work. Like Harry and Eddie before her, she was greatly challenged through Mr Johnston's weekly ministry at the Welcome Hall, and she also heard the pastor's call to surrender all to Jesus Christ. In response to God's call on her life, she entered the Faith Mission Training College in Edinburgh in 1958.

Besides employing her anointed talents as an evangelist with the Faith Mission, Betty was also gifted with a beautiful singing voice, which she frequently used to the glory of God. With her fellow Faith Mission workers Betty was instrumental in leading many people, young and old, to personal faith in Jesus Christ. She continued in that work until she was forced to return home because of her parents' health.

Betty related her own testimony:

Although I was not brought up in a 'church-going' family, I do remember my mother kneeling by my bed and praying with me. Her prayers were simple, but they still remain with me after all these years.

However, even though the Gospel message was foreign to me, a friend's granddad often stopped us on the street, took out his little New Testament and shared with us what he had been reading that morning. There were many other incidents in my life when I was confronted with the Gospel, but the biggest influence came when my brother Eddie got saved and shared his testimony with the family. As a result of his life and his encouragement I accepted the Lord Jesus Christ as my Saviour in the summer of 1949.

After my conversion Eddie introduced me to the Welcome Hall, which became my spiritual home. During those early years at the Welcome I sat at the feet of godly men and women who not only taught the Scriptures, but they also taught me how to pray with passion and intercede for the lost. The 'wee Welcome', as it was affectionately known to us, became the school where we learned to wait upon God, the place where men and women inspired us to go deeper with God.

Pastor Johnston was always there to make sure we never became rusty or redundant. 'Full salvation' and 'separation' were constantly drummed into our ears in the hope that it would touch, change and mould our hearts.

It was as a result of this wonderful fellowship and guidance that God's call came to my heart during the summer of 1956 when I spent a few days at Glenada, the YMCA centre in Newcastle, Co Down. While there I met four Faith Mission workers and supported them in their open-air witness at the town's sea-front promenade. Although God put His hand on my life at that time, I did not enter the Faith Mission College until 1958.

After the two years training in Edinburgh we were sent out into the evangelistic work of the mission. We went 'two by two', lived in small caravans during the summer and winter and conducted evangelistic missions in churches, mission halls, houses, tents and barns. Because we seldom had the benefit of electricity we had to be adept in lighting Tilley Lamps and firing potbelly coal stoves to heat the halls. We cycled all over the countryside visiting homes and farms within a radius of ten miles from where we were conducting the meetings and sometimes even farther.

As you may understand, this work was not easy, but we praise the Lord for those people who came to Christ and continue to follow Him until this very day. We praise God also that we have been able to see how the Lord has worked in many of these family circles even unto the third and fourth generation. Truly the Lord's service is amazing.

Although my heart was in the Faith Mission and the work I was enjoying, my mother's health deteriorated so much that I had no other choice but to leave the work I loved and return home in 1967. My mother's strength continued to decline until the Lord finally called her home in 1972.

Even though I was no longer engaged in a full-time capacity with the Faith Mission, I did continue to take part in various evangelistic missions and sang at the Faith Mission conferences and conventions until that God-given talent came to an end.

Life has moved on for me and so has my youth. I thank God for His faithfulness and love which have guided me as a Christian and Social Worker down through the years and finally into retirement.

As I have already indicated, my singing voice has long since gone, my preaching ministry has taken a back seat, but I am glad that I am able to encourage, support and pray for others who are now serving the Lord at home and abroad.

As Betty related in her testimony, she was always indebted to Pastor Jack Johnston and she gave her own recollection of her early days at the Welcome Hall:

Unlike some of the other folk who went to the Welcome Hall, I only go back to 1949 when, as a young child, I gave my heart to the Lord Jesus Christ and started to attend the Welcome Sunday School. I was in my middle to late teens before I really got to know and appreciate Mr Johnston. However, as I look back on those early years I can see his great influence upon my life. I really thank the Lord for the privilege of having such a godly man as an example when I was a teenager. His wisdom and counsel were especially a great help and encouragement to me when I felt God calling me into the Faith Mission.

For me, Pastor Johnston was the grandfather I never had, the guide I needed and a wise counsellor who enabled me to use my gifts wisely and for the glory of God. He steered all of us young people through the early years of our Christian experience and pressed upon us the importance of committing 'OUR ALL' to the Lord Jesus Christ. His favourite saying when speaking of the children of Israel going over the River Jordan was, 'Not a hoof was left behind. They went clean over the Jordan.' That is what he wanted for all of us.

Mr Johnston did not visit very many homes, but he was interested in all of our families. Although he was strict, he did have a good sense of humour and loved being in the midst of the young people. He was always there to encourage, rebuke and advise us. Sometimes he would slip into our Young People's meeting to make sure we were behaving properly, wearing our hats and not playing silly games.

A day out with Mr Johnston was always very interesting. No matter where we went or whatever was the occasion, he always had us end the day with an open-air meeting and distribution of Gospel tracts. He never missed an opportunity to witness for His Lord and testify of God's salvation. This was great training ground for us. Furthermore, he also taught us to make sure our work for God would be drenched in prayer.

We were constantly encouraged to speak to the visiting missionaries from different countries and various missionary societies and then pray for them. We were also treated to visits from the very best Bible teachers who were invited to open the Word of God for us and feed our souls.

Every year we had special evangelistic campaigns when gifted evangelists preached with passion. These special occasions each year only supplemented the weekly visits of various preachers who declared God's Word every Sunday throughout the year. Mr Johnston did not preach every week, but although he invited able men to teach the Bible, he was always in control. He guarded the pulpit from any error or falsehood. He was also quick to spot the gifts and talents of emerging young Christian workers amongst us and enthusiastically encouraged them to take part in various services.

The meetings at the Welcome Hall were never dull. They

were always very challenging. As I said before, Mr Johnston was very strict and was always in control of the meetings. Loud talking or jesting before or after the services was very much discouraged and if Mr Johnston thought that someone was idling away their time he gave them a job to do. He often quipped, 'Satan finds mischief for idle hands to do.'

The Welcome Hall was a family. We prayed together, played together and if anyone suffered, then we suffered together. Today we hear so much about "all-age worship" whatever that means, but Mr Johnston saw to it that we moved as one. There was no segregation or hiving off into little groups. The old and the young complemented each other, and we learned from each other as God moved amongst us night after night.

The Welcome Hall was Mr Johnston, and Mr Johnston was the Welcome Hall. The two were inseparable and had one heart.

I can only describe Mr Johnston by saying, 'There was a man sent from God…'

CHAPTER 17

A New Chapter

A decision was made in 1959 to finally pull down Amy's Tin Tabernacle and build a new structure. Kate Mitchell's purchase of the prefabricated building had been a great investment. During the seventy years since its opening that simple building had seen the conversion of hundreds of people through Pastor Johnston's ministry. Added to that, countless numbers of Christians had been blessed and nurtured in their spiritual lives and many servants of God sent off to serve God in other places.

However, an improving economic situation in the country meant that times were changing and the old corrugated building was not very becoming for the growing congregation at the Welcome Hall and a more affluent age. A decision was therefore made to erect a more permanent and appropriate structure.

Pastor Johnston had been praying and planning for this new building for many years. He and Mrs Johnston had opened a building fund account fifteen years earlier in the hope that someday 'Amy's Tin Tabernacle' would be replaced with a more permanent building.

Other changes were also afoot. With his advancing years Pastor Johnston's ability and strength was diminishing. He was no longer able to carry the responsibility of continuing to lead the work of the Welcome Hall. In 1961 Mr Johnston suggested to the trustees that Mr Teddy Allen, one of the faithful workers at the Hall, be recognised as the assistant Superintendent of the Welcome Hall to help him in the work. This was duly accepted and as Mr Johnston's role gradually diminished, Ted Allen was able to step in to oversee the work until a new pastor was appointed.

Before his death, Pastor Johnston was able to witness the opening of the new building on 5th September 1959. Miss Mitchell's niece, Mrs K Brownrigg, declared the new hall open for the glory of God and Mr Rene Thompson chaired the meeting that followed.

The total cost of the new structure came to around £5,500.00. The offering taken that opening day cleared any outstanding debt that had accumulated during the months of construction. The new church was opened free from debt.

Sam Morrow, who attended the Welcome for many years, wrote the following tribute to the work of the Welcome Hall:

The Old Welcome Hall

The Old Welcome Hall has been taken down
Which has stood for seventy years,
Where many have the Saviour found
With broken heart and tears.
And many have been obedient
And answered the Saviour's call
And went out to serve as missionaries
From the Old Welcome Hall.

The Old Welcome Hall has served its time.
They have built a new one in its place,
But many souls still live and shine
As trophies of God's grace.
Because they learned at Sunday School
When they were children small;
The wondrous love of Jesus
That was taught in the Old Welcome Hall.

If the Old Welcome Hall could only speak
What a story it would tell,
Of sinners who did the Saviour seek
When He saved their soul from hell.
They enjoyed sweet peace and fellowship,
And many times I recall,
When the Lord came down and blessed us
In the Old Welcome Hall.

The meeting for opening the new hall was a thrilling day and a fitting climax for Pastor Johnston's work. That building still stands today as a monument and memorial of that faithful servant of God.

The people at the Welcome were asking for God to indicate who the new pastor should be. They were not aware that in a wonderful way God had already planned that the man of His choice to take Pastor Johnston's place would be available at the right time.

In 1959 Robert and Isobel Mackey and family were at home after serving the Lord with the WEC in Liberia for nearly twenty years. Although for a few years they had been helping at a Bible College near Holywood, County Down, they were still unsettled about their future ministry. At a meeting of the trustees of the Welcome in September 1964 it was decided that that an approach should be made to Robert Mackey inviting him to fill the pastoral vacancy at the Welcome Hall.

At that same meeting of the trustees when the invitation was extended to Robert Mackey to be pastor and superintendent of the Welcome Hall, a letter from Mr Johnston was read in which Jack Johnston tendered his resignation as superintendent in view of his failing health. The minutes of the meeting record that this resignation was "accepted regretfully".

Following the reading of Mr Johnston's resignation the Chairman, Mr Rene Thompson, paid an eloquent tribute to Mr Johnston and his thirty-eight years of dedicated ministry at the Welcome Hall. An extract from the minutes of the meeting states:

> The Chairman paid tribute to the magnificent work Mr Johnston had done over the past thirty-eight years and asked that this be recorded in the minutes. It was also agreed that he should be invited to act as a consultant after his retirement as Superintendent. It was also agreed that he should be allowed to retain a key to give him access to the Welcome Hall for his Quiet Times.

At the same meeting of the Trustees Mr Teddy Allen also tendered his resignation as assistant superintendent at the Welcome Hall. Teddy had worked very well alongside Pastor Johnston over the previous three years, but in view of the coming changes he felt he should step down to allow Pastor Mackey to have a freehand in the leadership of the work. Both Pastor Johnston and Teddy Allen gave the new pastor their full support and remained active until Pastor Mackey was able to assume his full responsibilities.

Robert and Isobel Mackey felt that the Lord was behind the

invitation from the trustees and on 1ˢᵗ December 1964 Robert was inducted into the beginning of his ministry at the Welcome Hall. The congregation at the Welcome Hall were so glad that a man of God and an experienced missionary had been installed as the new pastor a few months before Mr Johnston was taken home to heaven.

In the providence of God Pastor Johnston's time alongside the new pastor was very limited. The former pastor's devotional times with the Lord in the quietness of the Welcome Hall soon gave way to his departure to be with Christ. Bobby and Tilley Snodden looked after Pastor Johnston at their Olive Street home until he laid aside his earthly tabernacle and went to his heavenly house on the 25th April, 1966. Everyone at the Hall felt it was so appropriate that he had gone home to heaven from the Snoddon's front bedroom. Bobby and Tilly were with him to the very last when he made a triumphant entrance into heaven.

Pastor Johnston had a full and blessed life most of which had been dedicated to the work and witness at the Welcome Hall. At his funeral service it was noted that the work might have completely disappeared had it not been for the vision, dedication and faithful Bible ministry of Jack and Elizabeth Johnston. While his passing was greatly lamented by his friends at the Welcome Hall, they knew that he had received a far greater 'welcome' as a good and faithful servant of the Lord.

Pastor Robert Mackey and his wife Isobel

CHAPTER 18

God's Man

Over the next five years Pastor Mackey gave excellent leadership to the congregation and introduced several changes for the benefit of the work at the Welcome Hall. One of the first things he did was to formulate a list of the members. Until then there had not been a formal membership role at the Hall. The Welcome was simply looked upon as a local fellowship of Christians committed to God's work. Those who belonged to the Hall had always considered it to be their spiritual home but had never been received in as members. Initially, Pastor Mackey was able to enlist thirty-six believers who wished to register as members of the Hall.

With the permission of the trustees, Robert Mackey was also able to establish a 'management committee' which would act as a board of elders at the Welcome although they would be subject and accountable to the trustees. The first management committee comprised of Pastor Mackey, Roy Kernaghan, Robert Crawford, Jim Whyte and Billy Lyttle.

Following the drawing up of a membership role, in 1966 Pastor Robert Mackey encouraged the trustees to consider changing the status of the Welcome Hall as a mission hall to become the Welcome Hall Church. Up to that time, although the Welcome Hall had functioned as a church, it was generally looked upon as a mission. This proposal from Pastor Mackey was met with some resistance at first, but after Robert Mackey's counsel it was eventually accepted by the trustees. Alongside this change of status, Pastor Mackey also successfully encouraged the trustees to apply to the Belfast Registrar for the Welcome Hall Church to be authorised to conduct weddings on its premises.

It was also through Pastor Mackey's leadership in 1968 that the Welcome Hall became a member of the Fellowship of Independent Evangelical Churches (FIEC), and its name was consequently changed to the Welcome Evangelical Church.

It was near the end of Robert Mackey's tenure at the Welcome Hall that riots broke out at the Protestant/Catholic interface on the nearby Crumlin Road. These riots were the beginnings of terrorist violence and civil unrest that would afflict Northern Ireland and Great Britain for the next forty years. This period, a terrible and bloody stain on Ulster's history, became known as "The Troubles".

In June 1969, just a few weeks before the outbreak of those far-reaching riots, Pastor Mackey sounded out a timely message in his editorial of the Welcome Evangelical Church's magazine:

We wondered what would come next. Now the secret is out. It is to be A PROGRAMME OF CIVIL DISOBEDIENCE. Amusing! Like pouting kids, the prime movers for civil rights must have WHAT they want and WHEN they want it, or they will pursue a course of civil wrongs with total disregard for law and order.

One thing we are assured of: CIVIL DISOBEDIENCE does not have to be added to any human programme; it is there already and has been for a very long time. In fact, it was nothing less that brought ruin to the race for, and I quote Paul,

'By one man's DISOBEDIENCE many were made sinners.' Long practised in this art man needs neither reminding nor instructing. DISOBEDIENCE is already part of his nature and given half a chance, will always lend hearty support any time it is called for.

Bear this in mind: it is never right to do wrong, - and disobedience is just that. Therefore, to be right and promote right, and thus please a righteous God, the Christian must plant his feet firmly in His Master's footsteps and tread the path of obedience. Of Him it is said, 'He... became OBEDIENT unto death, even the death of the cross' (Philippians 2:8). And the outcome? 'By the OBEDIENCE of One many shall be made RIGHTeous.'

Disobedience is characteristic of the first Adam; obedience is characteristic of the last. Each carries its own reward. With the former goes blight and barreness; with the latter blessing and abundance. The choice is always before you. Set your heart to obey, for 'if ye will be willing and OBEDIENT, ye shall eat the good of the land' (Isaiah 1:19).

This editorial was a salutary warning to the young people in the Cambrai Street community who were very vulnerable to being sucked into extremist activities during the terrorist campaign that followed. Sadly, too many young people from the district were drawn into paramilitary organisations and consequently ended up on the wrong side of the law and behind bars. Worse still, others became victims of the most horrendous, brutal and murderous acts of violence, which were indiscriminately wreaked upon the wider community.

One such victim of these troubles was Jimmy Stewart. Like

many other young men from the upper Shankill, Jimmy was converted to Jesus Christ during Mr Mackey's pastorate. He was born nearby in Oregon Street, and although reared into a Christian home, he strayed from the teachings of the Scriptures and sowed his wild oats during his youthful years. One night Jimmy's mother invited him to a Gospel meeting in the Welcome Hall to hear Robert Mackey preach. God opened his heart to the Gospel on that night, 29th September 1968.

During the next four years Jimmy Stewart integrated into the fellowship at the Welcome Hall and quickly matured in his Christian life. Sadly, tragedy struck Jimmy and some other unsuspecting people on Saturday afternoon, 4th March, 1972. It had always been Jimmy's custom to visit the city centre every Saturday for shopping. On that particular day, after completing his purchases, Jimmy dropped into the popular Abercorn Restaurant for a relaxing cup of tea.

While seated at a table with many other Saturday shoppers, a horrendous explosion suddenly ripped through the building. The deafening roar was followed by clouds of dust filling the air and falling debris landing around Jimmy. The restaurant was plunged into darkness, but out of that darkness agonising yells and painful screams of the injured victims penetrated the air. The interior of the restaurant was like a war scene. Windows were blown out; the ceiling had fallen down, and splintered furniture was scattered all over the dining area. Worse still, the terrible blast had left two women dead and 139 people maimed or seriously injured. Many of these injuries included the loss of limbs and eyes. Among those seriously injured was Jimmy Stewart of the Welcome Hall.

Although no organisation ever claimed responsibility, and none was ever charged in connection with the bombing, it was unofficially acknowledged that terrorists from the Provisional Irish Republican Army were responsible. Jimmy said afterwards that all he could remember of that terrible day was the horrific sound of the blast while he sat at a table drinking tea.

That's all I remembered for some days, until the surgeon broke the awful news to me, 'I am sorry Mr Stewart, but there was absolutely nothing we could do--both legs had to be amputated above the knees.'

I just couldn't believe it. The bottom seemed to have fallen out of my world. The thought came to me, *Why me Lord? Do I have to spend the rest of my life in a wheel chair, a helpless and hopeless cripple?*

As I lay in the hospital bed, after the surgeon left, I was crushed, grief stricken and bewildered. It was then that the Saviour drew graciously close with reassuring words, 'I will never leave thee. My grace is sufficient for thee.'

I reached out to Him in my need, and the joy of the Lord flooded my soul. I felt as though I had been transported to heaven. I knew from that moment forward that all would be well. I can now say years later that the Lord has kept His word.

Within two years not only was Jimmy able to walk, but he was able to walk up the short aisle at the Welcome Evangelical Church to be married to his beautiful fiancée, Miss Florence Orr. Jimmy was no longer alone. God had provided a companion and helpmeet for him.

Late in 1969 the leadership of the WEC came looking for the services of Robert and Isobel Mackey. Subsequently, Robert was appointed to be the British General Secretary of the WEC with a worldwide ministry. The people at the Welcome were sorry to see Robert and Isobel leave, but they knew this couple was well suited to a far wider ministry on various mission fields. During their five years at the Welcome the membership had not only been formalised, it had also increased considerably.

A meeting of the Welcome Hall trustees recorded the announcement of Robert Mackey's departure from his leadership role at the Welcome:

> The Chairman spoke of the sad event, which brought us together this evening, namely the resignation of Rev Robert Mackey as pastor. He was shortly to go to be General Secretary of the Worldwide Evangelisation Crusade for the United Kingdom. He believed that the Lord had called Mr Mackey to this work and all present agreed that such was the position. Expressions of appreciation were made by various members for Mr Mackey's service over the last five years. The question of a successor was also mentioned and Mr Mackey named several people who might be suitable for the position. It was suggested that he should write to these people and invite them to speak at the Welcome Evangelical Church.

Robert and Isobel Mackey finished their ministry at the Welcome with a special Farewell Service on Saturday, 27th December 1969. On the following day he preached his farewell sermon.

Mr Ray Peers, an English evangelist and a former student at the WEC Missionary Training College in Glasgow, was invited to conduct the services at the Welcome for the first two months of 1970.

CHAPTER 19

Changes

No servant of God finds the Lord's work to be easy, nor does it advance without opposition, problems and frustrations. Even the great Apostle Paul found that with every open door comes adversity. The Welcome Hall Church was not exempt from its share of problems and frustrations. Perhaps some of this was due to Pastor Johnston having conducted such a long and settled ministry spanning almost forty years. For thirty-five years he was a father figure to the congregation, had led most of the members to faith in Jesus Christ and nurtured them in the faith. During all those years the Welcome Hall had not been accustomed to transitions from one pastor to another.

Pastor Robert Mackey brought much of the benefit of his years of missionary experience to the Welcome Hall, and this helped make a smooth transition to organising it into the Welcome Evangelical Church with its registered own membership. He further introduced measures for the church to become a member of the Fellowship of Independent Evangelical Churches.

Following Ray Peers' short ministry at the Welcome during the early months of 1970, the responsibility for the on-going work rested on the shoulders of the Management Committee, which Robert Mackay had established previously. They invited various speakers to preach at the Hall each week and the members rallied round to support the elders in their work.

In October of that same year, two well-known Ulster evangelists, Mr Matt Boland and Mr Noel Grant from Bangor, conducted a very successful evangelistic mission at the Welcome Evangelical Church. During those weeks quite a number of people were converted, including a local schoolteacher. However, that same year closed without any further indication of a possible replacement for the pastoral vacancy. During the course of the next year the trustees and the members earnestly engaged in prayer for God's guidance to find the man of His choice, but at the end of 1971 the vacancy still persisted.

It was in May 1972 that the trustees reported that they all felt that Mr John Galbraith, a student at the Irish Baptist College in Belfast, was the person who should be invited to fill the vacancy. The trustees of the Welcome Evangelical Church called for a members' meeting to make a decision about inviting Pastor John Galbraith to become their pastor. Pastor Galbraith's appointment was overwhelmingly endorsed at that meeting.

John Galbraith was a member of Connsbrook Congregational Church in East Belfast, and although he still had another year of his college studies to complete, he was willing to accept the invitation while he continued his studies. Pastor John Galbraith, who became pastor more than two years after Pastor Mackey left, remained at the Welcome for only two years. Although Pastor Galbraith addressed his work with zealous evangelistic endeavour, some differences of opinion arose amongst the fellowship in relation to his Bible teaching. In view of these disagreements Pastor Galbraith and a few other leading members stepped down from their positions in September 1973. Within a short time Pastor Galbraith received an invitation to become the pastor at East End Baptist Church on the other side of the city.

By this time Amy Carmichael had already gone to be with Christ. In the book, *A Very Present Help: Life Messages of Great Christians,* Amy had written, "The best training is to learn to accept everything as it comes, as from Him whom our soul loves. The tests are always unexpected things, not great things that can be written up, but the common little rubs of life, silly little nothings, things you are ashamed of minding one scrap." How true this was in what seemed to be the unexpected setbacks in the work at the Welcome Evangelical Church.

With the sudden departure of Pastor Galbraith Mr Billy Lyttle, one of the elders at the Welcome Evangelical Church from Pastor Mackey's time, stepped in to fill the leadership role. With the help of the other elders he kept the work going until a new pastor could be found.

God's timing is always perfect. Eddie and Sadie Young were obliged to return home from Senegal in 1979 after twenty years of service with WEC International. Before leaving Africa they were not sure what the future held for them. While Eddie and Sadie were busy on deputation work for the WEC the leadership at the Welcome Hall Church saw that Eddie was ideally suited to become the new pastor of the flock. It was under the ministry of Pastor Johnston at the Welcome that Eddie had been nurtured in his Christian life. Until he left for Bible College in 1951 Eddie had been very active in the Gospel outreach into the area alongside Mr Johnston. Furthermore, the church had supported Eddie and Sadie for almost thirty years.

After Pastor Galbraith left the Welcome Evangelical Church,

Eddie was available to help with the weekly ministry at the Hall during the last few months of 1979. His preaching was not only very acceptable but many spoke of how they had been blessed in the meetings. There was no doubt with the trustees or members that Eddie and Sadie Young should be invited to lead the work at the Welcome Evangelical Church.

Accordingly, Eddie was invited to fill the vacancy. He recognised that God's hand was in this invitation and consented to become the new pastor at the Welcome Evangelical Church. He was inducted as pastor 5th January 1980 and for the next seventeen years Eddie and Sadie faithfully served the Welcome Evangelical Church.

During those years Pastor Young continued to stimulate missionary interest at the church and organised many Gospel missions. These missions were conducted by various evangelists including Ivan Thompson, Patrick Kitchen, Rev. Sam Workman and George Bates. In all these missions many people were converted to Jesus Christ.

However, Eddie and the friends at the Hall were aware that they were engaged in spiritual warfare. This was manifestly evident one night during the mission conducted by George Bates in 1981. Before the meeting started, a well-dressed young lady, carrying a Bible and a notebook, took a seat adjacent to the aisle. As the meeting got under way the lady joined in with the rest of the congregation to sing the hymns and choruses. All seemed normal and the Lord gave George great liberty in his preaching. His subject for the evening was "The Soul that God gives up".

After he had expounded his message George made an appeal for people to publicly acknowledge their need and come to Christ. Suddenly and without any warning, there was a change of atmosphere. It seemed as if all hell was let loose on the meeting. The young lady suddenly started to scream at the top of her voice and in different vocal tones. At the same time she began throwing items into the air; her hymnbook, her Bible and her handbag were scattered over the congregation. She even grabbed the chair beside her and made an attempt to throw it also. The atmosphere was electrified. Nothing like this had ever happened at the Welcome before. Women who sat near her shrunk for cover while George and Pastor Eddie Young moved in to try and control her. They had difficulty in doing so for the young woman was so strong as she tried to persist in her demonic behaviour.

After much fervent prayer with the help of God, the two men were finally able to restore the woman to a form of normality. This was an undoubted attack from the devil. However, God had the victory that night for the same woman and four other people were counselled for salvation at the end of the eventful evening. When all was finished George and Eddie finally got the woman to her home. During the trip home she kept singing many of the choruses they had been singing in the meeting earlier that evening. During that evangelistic mission seventeen people were saved and quite a few backsliders were restored.

Having served the Lord through seventeen very eventful and fruitful years at the Welcome, Eddie and Sadie felt that they should stand down from active ministry at the Hall and make way for a suitable replacement. They did not take this step lightly, but they were convinced that it was time for a change.

In the following year, 1998, the elders approached Jim Thompson and invited him to be the new pastor of the Welcome. After some deliberation Jim and his wife Sarah, felt this was the right step for them and for the next two years Pastor Jim Thompson led the ministry at the Welcome.

After Jim left the pastorate in 2000 the elders at the Welcome had to face the challenge of searching for a new pastor. Eventually they were introduced to John and Gwyneth Miskelly. John had previously been the minister at Ballynahinch Congregational Church, but after the approach of the elders from the Welcome he decided to accept the invitation to be the new pastor at the Cambrai Street Church.

It was during Pastor Miskelly's time at the Welcome that a decision was taken to erect a hall on a piece of land at the side of the church. This was needed for the Sunday School and a place to which the workers of the church could bring young people off the street. This prefabricated building of equal dimensions as those of the main church, was opened to the glory of God in 2003. It was erected in memory of Pastor Johnston and became known as "The Johnston Memorial Hall". The building came complete with a store, toilets and a kitchen besides the main hall. Since its opening this hall has been put to good use as an outreach centre into the community.

Pastor John Miskelly vacated his position as pastor at the Welcome Evangelical Church in 2002. Although Pastor Eddie Young had officially retired from his position at the Welcome in 1997 he was soon reinstated again for another three years when the elders and trustees at the church failed to find a suitable replacement.

Sadie Young was a source of constant support and encouragement at Eddie's side throughout their years of service for Christ in Africa and at the Welcome. Sadie went to be with the Lord on 22nd July 2012. Eddie still worships at the Welcome Evangelical Church until this present time.

CHAPTER 20

Shepherds and Labourers

The Welcome Evangelical Church was full to capacity for the evening service on Sunday, 28th May 2006. Many visitors joined the congregation to witness the induction of a young man to the ministry of the church. An atmosphere of expectation and excitement pervaded the meeting. The people of the Welcome had been praying for a man of God's choice to be their pastor and they believed this was an answer to those prayers. Eddie Young, the former pastor at the Welcome, led the proceedings. This was most appropriate for he was passing on the baton of leadership at the Welcome to a younger man, Jonathan Clarke, who was embarking on his second pastorate. Prior to this appointment Jonathan had been pastor of Randalstown Elim Church for three years.

Lorraine, Jonathan's wife, sat beside their four-year-old son, Joel. Her mind lurched from one emotion to another, sometimes looking forward to this step with a fair measure of anticipation, but her hopes were always tempered and cautioned with an equal amount of apprehension as she contemplated the new challenge ahead.

Notwithstanding the responsibilities that lay before him, Jonathan listened intently as his good friend, David Christie, opened the meeting with prayer for Jonathan and his family at the outset of this new venture. David had been a big influence on Jonathan's life and always had timely words of encouragement for Jonathan and Lorraine. With characteristic poise and godly demeanour, David prayed for God's richest blessings to be on the new pastor and the congregation.

Jonathan knew that he would need those blessings for he was facing a daunting challenge. Church attendance in the Shankill Road area had greatly decreased and was still diminishing. Some churches had reduced their Sunday activities to morning service only and some nearby mission halls had closed down. Furthermore, the congregation at the Welcome Evangelical Church did not have many young people. However, Jonathan also knew that God had called him and he felt he could do no other than to accept the challenge that was before him.

After Eddie Young gave a message in which he outlined the responsibilities of a pastor Jonathan was invited to speak. After some expressions of gratitude to the church for the confidence they had placed in him by inviting him to be their new pastor, he read from his Bible in Acts 16:22-34. He announced to the congregation that he was facing a challenge he could not avoid or run away from. He knew God had clearly called him. At the same time, he was not unaware of how daunting and great the challenge was. He told them that as he had pondered these responsibilities God had drawn him to the account of the conversion of the Philippian jailor as recorded in his Bible reading. Jonathan then disclosed his theme; "It Took an Earthquake." The new pastor went on to enlarge on this theme and indicated that the God who shook that jail was still the same today. The Gospel that led to the conversion of that unlikely convert had still the same dynamic today and the grace that reached the jailor's family was still available to reach the people of the Shankill community today.

Jonathan's message was dynamic, encouraging and inspiring.

The people at the Welcome Church were delighted to learn that Jonathan Clarke was reared nearby in Rathlin Street, which is only one block away from the church. That meant that their new pastor was a local lad who knew the neighbourhood and his family was well known in the local community. Both of his Christian parents had been born and reared on the mid-Shankill. After Pastor Ravey had married them at Shankill Baptist Church in 1960, they had bought a house and settled in the Woodvale Road area.

With their move to the Woodvale area Mr & Mrs Clarke began to attend Woodvale Methodist Church. However, their three Clarke children, Jonathan, his older sister Lorraine, and older brother Dessie, still attended Sunday School at Zion Tabernacle in Canmore Street, which was near their parents' former homes. It was at the Zion Tabernacle that Jonathan was first taught the way of salvation through Jesus Christ. Church also played a part in the family's life. Lorraine joined the Girl's Guides at Woodvale Methodist while Jonathan enrolled in the church's Boys Brigade Company. However, in spite of all the Christian influence at home, at church and the Bible teaching at the Sunday School, Jonathan still had not received Jesus Christ as personal Saviour.

When he finally was converted everything changed. His brother Dessie arrived home one Sunday evening to announce to the family that he had been converted. Although this was an answer to his parent's prayers it was a shock to his sixteen-year-old brother, Jonathan. It made a sudden and massive impact on Jonathan's life. He had been unexpectedly awakened to think of his own spiritual need. Previously he had been aware of that need, but too often he had tried to deny it or run away from it. Now he was confronted with the impact of his brother's conversion.

Added to this, Dessie immediately engaged in witnessing

about his newfound faith by inviting Jonathan to a youth event associated with the Whitewell Metropolitan Tabernacle, which is on the outskirts of Belfast. Jonathan knew that what had happened to Dessie was not only what he needed, but deep down in his heart, it was what he wanted. However, fear and doubt hindered him from taking that step. He was afraid of what people might say and afraid that he would not be able to live up to being a Christian.

Those fears were swept away at the evening service at Whitewell Metropolitan Tabernacle on Sunday evening, 12th October 1986. After the Glengormerly Methodist Youth Choir sang out a clear Gospel message with great sincerity, Jonathan listened to Pastor James McConnell powerfully preach the Gospel of the Lord Jesus Christ. No longer could he resist the Holy Spirit's striving in his heart. Jonathan realised as never before that if he continued to reject Jesus Christ he could be lost for all eternity. He could delay no longer in accepting Jesus Christ. As soon as the preacher pronounced the benediction at the close of the service Jonathan rose from his seat in the church's upper balcony and began to make his way along the aisle, down the stairs and then make his way to the front of the church. As he went he felt as though he was being swept along in a mixture of a gripping conviction of sin and deep contrition in his heart. Thank God, on that night Jonathan Clarke accepted Jesus Christ as personal Saviour.

Jonathan's earlier fears of confessing Christ to others were soon overcome when he told his parents of his decision. God also enabled him to speak to others about the Saviour. It was obvious that Jonathan was fired with the same Christian zeal and enthusiasm that had seized his brother Dessie. Jonathan immediately became involved in street outreach and door-to-door evangelism. He was invited to help in various youth events at the church and young people's meetings.

CHAPTER 21

Welcome to The Welcome

During those early days after his conversion Jonathan Clarke struck up a friendship with other Christian young people who shared a hunger for more of God's blessing on their lives. Besides attending the weekly church prayer meeting, these young men met for extra seasons of prayer. Quite a few of those young men from that group are in active Christian service today.

In the process of time Jonathan was invited to testify publicly in various meetings about his conversion to Jesus Christ. On several occasions he even ventured to preach at a various meetings. However, the more Jonathan witnessed and testified, the more he felt his need to study the Word of God. Like all new Christians, it seemed as if the Bible had become a new book for him; it was his daily bread to feed his soul. Reading the Bible created in him a deeper hunger to learn more about God's Word.

Jonathan's desire for more Bible study prompted him to enrol in the Elim Bible College Course for Christian Workers, which was being taught at Hillsborough Elim Church. Besides greatly benefitting from his two years course at the college Jonathan also came under the tutelage of Pastor Robert McAvoy who was pastor at Randalstown Elim Church at that time. Pastor McAvoy not only became Jonathan's mentor, he also invited Jonathan to work with him as a youth pastor at the Randalstown church. It was then that Jonathan began to develop his ability to preach at various meetings.

Prior to enrolling for the Bible College course Jonathan had been employed at O'Hara's Bakery in Belfast. It was there that he had another life-changing experience. It was at the bakery that Jonathan met Lorraine Boreland who came from the nearby Highfield Housing Estate, which is just off the Ballygomartin Road. Lorraine caught Jonathan's eye, and within a short time she had completely stolen his heart. He was glad when he discovered that Lorraine had been converted the very same week that he also had trusted the Lord Jesus. Jonathan did not need a lot of encouragement to ask Lorraine to go out with him on a date and was glad when she readily accepted his invitation.

That initial date led to a two and a half year courtship for Jonathan and Lorraine. The happy couple were finally married at the Whitewell Metropolitan Tabernacle on Saturday, 30th August 1997. The day of their memorable wedding was overshadowed with another momentous event in the early hours of the next morning when the nation and the world were suddenly thrown into deep shock and mourning with the tragic death of Princess Diana in Paris. Today when people speak of Princess Diana's death with great sadness Jonathan and Lorraine do not have to be reminded that they have other happy memories of that same weekend.

Jonathan and Lorraine set up home on Rutherglen Street which is on the Ballygomartin Road. The Lord greatly blessed and enriched their home with the birth of their son, Joel, on 7th November 2001.

In 2003 when Jonathan was employed as a service technician with Initial he was inducted as pastor at Randalstown Elim church after the departure of Pastor Robert McAvoy. For the next three years Jonathan gained valuable experience as he engaged in his weekly Bible ministry.

Early in 2006 Jonathan became acquainted with Pastor Dennis Murphy who had recently been installed as the pastor at Ballygomartin Baptist Church. At that time Jonathan had already stepped down from being pastor at Randalstown. While he began to evaluate his life and his future ministry he was constrained to throw his weight into the work at the nearby Baptist church with Dennis Murphy.

Only a few weeks after he had made this decision to attend Ballygomartin Baptist Church Jonathan came to know Pastor Eddie Young who had recently retired from his ministry at the Welcome Evangelical Church. Eddie invited Jonathan to conduct the Sunday services at the Welcome. For Jonathan, this was an amazing experience. He had always been burdened and concerned for the working class people of the upper Shankill, the area where he had been reared.

Jonathan enjoyed the visit to the Welcome, and afterwards he was invited back for other Sunday preaching engagements. Following these visits Eddie Young approached him on behalf of the congregation and asked if he would consider becoming their pastor. At first, Jonathan declined the invitation. He felt he should not make another sudden change in his life since he had only recently started to attend the Ballygomartin Baptist Church. At the same time, Dennis Murphy encouraged Jonathan to give further consideration to this opening at the Welcome. He counselled Jonathan that if the Lord was behind this invitation to the Welcome, then the Lord would speak to him again.

That is exactly what happened. One Saturday in 2006, while Jonathan was making his final preparations to preach on the following day, he was struck with the final verses of Matthew 9:35-37; "And Jesus went about all the cities and villages, teaching in their synagogues, and preaching the Gospel of the kingdom, and healing every sickness and every disease among the people. But when he saw the multitudes, he was moved with compassion on them, because they fainted, and were scattered abroad, as sheep having no shepherd. Then saith he unto his disciples, 'The harvest truly is plenteous, but the labourers are few; Pray ye therefore the Lord of the harvest, that he will send forth labourers into his harvest.'"

The words, "The multitudes... fainting... scattered... no shepherd... the labourers are few," greatly impacted Jonathan's heart and mind. He remembered the district where he had been reared and the multitudes that still lived on the narrow streets between the Shankill and the Crumlin Roads.

Although Jonathan tried to continue with his sermon preparation he could not escape from the challenge that had come to him that Saturday evening. *Could this be God speaking again,* he wondered. He recalled his earlier concern for the neighbourhood where he had been raised. *Lord, do you want me to go back to work in the Shankill,* he prayed.

During the previous thirty years Shankill Road neighbourhood had suffered greatly because of the on-going terrorist campaign that had been cruelly inflicted on Ulster. Besides the destruction that had been left in the wake of more than three decades of the terrorist's scourge, the demolition of houses and reallocation of the population had seriously changed the demographics of the area. Consequently, churches and mission halls had suffered greatly and countless Sunday schools were depleted or closed. This had seemed almost unthinkable for the same area had been known for multiple open-air meetings, churches galore and mission halls peppered all over the district. Now a whole generation of children had grown up when families, perhaps afraid to allow their children to go far from home, no longer sent their boys and girls to Sunday School nor took them to church.

All Jonathan could think about was what he had read that evening: "multitudes... without a shepherd... the labourers are few". He responded in the quietness of his heart, "Lord, with your help, I will be a labourer for you among this people."

Convinced this was the voice of God speaking to him, Jonathan phoned Eddie Young the next morning, Sunday morning and told him, "Eddie, the Lord has spoken to me about going to the Welcome Evangelical Church, and I just want you to know that if the congregation issues a call I am prepared to give a positive answer."

Eddie set the wheels moving and within a short time the trustees at the Welcome issued an invitation to Jonathan to become their pastor. David Clarke, an elder at the Welcome, gave Jonathan and Lorraine the right hand of fellowship to welcome them to this new chapter in their lives and that of the Welcome Evangelical Church.

Times have changed since the days of the Shawlies when Amy Carmichael first caught the vision of erecting the old iron hall. The intervening years brought much blessing to the Welcome Hall through the ministry of various servants of God. Thousands of people have been brought to Christ through the influence of God's servants from the Welcome Evangelical Church. The text that Amy Carmichael chose for the wall above the pulpit still is given its prominent place and it still holds true, "That in all things He might have the pre-eminence."

Right from the outset of his ministry Jonathan brought much enthusiasm to his work. That enthusiasm was infectious. Members at the church were keen to help. On Thursday evenings some joined Jonathan in door-to-door visitation in the Woodvale area to invite people to the services. The Johnston Memorial Hall at the side of the church was put to good use to host young people on Saturday and Sunday evenings. This was a new chapter for Jonathan and Lorraine Clarke and a new start for the Welcome Evangelical Church.

Pastor J. Clarke at the launch of two Amy Carmichael DVDs in 2011

CHAPTER 22

Meet a Member

Ruth Carson's whole life has revolved around the Hall and the people who attended the Welcome over many years. She is typical of the people who have trusted Christ through the ministry of the Gospel at the Welcome Hall. Ruth is now the oldest member of the Welcome Evangelical Church. Ruth Dickson, as she was known in her childhood days, was reared around the corner from the Welcome in Leopold Street. This ninety-year-old lady has been attending the Welcome since she was five years of age. Despite her advanced years Ruth's mind is as clear as a bell and she is able to recall those early days in the mid-1920s when a young Mr Johnston embarked on his daunting mission to re-open "Amy's Tin Tabernacle" in Cambrai Street.

Ruth remembers that although Mr Johnston was a compassionate missionary, he was also very strict and kept very tight reigns on all that went on in the Welcome.

Ruth first attended the Sunday School in the simple hall with dozens of other boys and girls. On some Sundays a few mischievous boys from the locality who did not go to Sunday School ran along the side of the corrugated iron hall and with a stick in their hand. They pulled the stick along the building and as it thumped over the corrugated bumps it created a staccato roar inside, thus disturbing the Sunday School class. A very agile Mr Johnston was soon on their tail, not just to stop their impish behaviour, but to recruit them for the Sunday School. He was always on the lookout to win boys and girls for the Saviour.

When she was fourteen years old, Ruth and a friend ventured into an evangelistic meeting at Crumlin Road Presbyterian Church. At the end of that meeting Ruth knew that she needed to be saved. Sadly, there was no one to instruct her in the way of salvation after the meeting. However, Ruth knew that her granny was a Christian, and she would tell her what to do. Later, the kindly grandma was able to lead her granddaughter to faith in Christ.

Mr Johnston, always quick to find jobs for the teenagers at the Welcome, asked Ruth to teach a junior Sunday School class when she was seventeen years old. Within a short while Ruth was invited to take over the leadership of the young ladies' Bible Class as there was a vacancy. This was a big step and an equally huge challenge for Ruth, but over the next few years she was able to build up a great relationship with these girls who were aged seventeen through twenty-one years.

Besides teaching the Scriptures on Sundays, Ruth took treated her girls on outings for picnics and other social events at local seaside resorts. Ruth also organised her girls' class into a testimony team, and soon they were invited to conduct meetings in local churches and mission halls. At these meetings the girls sang and related their testimonies before Ruth gave a devotional or Gospel message. Both Ruth and the girls were delighted at one meeting when two ladies were led to faith in Jesus Christ.

It was also through her work with the Bible Class at the Welcome Hall that Ruth Dickson met William Carson, a young man from the Donegall Road area of Belfast who had started attending the Hall. Mr Johnston knew that the best way to secure the loyalty of young people was to recruit them for a job. Therefore, not long after William arrived at the Welcome, Mr Johnston found a Sunday School class for him to teach.

Very soon William and Ruth were going out for walks and on dates. Subsequently, William and Ruth were married in 1943 and set up home in Rosebank Street, which was near to the Welcome Hall. William and Ruth remained active members of the Welcome Hall for the rest of their lives until William passed away in May 1978.

William and Ruth Carson's children, David, Joy and Pauline, also trusted Christ as Saviour through the witness of the Welcome Hall. Their daughter Joy became the organist at the church while their son David became superintendent of the Sunday School. David and Stephen, Ruth's grandson, are present day trustees of the Welcome Evangelical Church.

The membership at the Welcome over the years has been made up of ordinary people whose lives were transformed by the power of the Gospel. Under the leadership of a succession of pastors these Christians have banded together to make sure that in all things Jesus Christ should always have the pre-eminence just as Amy intended at the outset of her work. They have been committed to maintaining the work and witness of Amy's "Tin Tabernacle" for more than a hundred years. In the providence of God and by His grace they are committed to make sure this work will continue until Jesus Christ returns for His church as He has promised.

The Welcome Evangelical Church 2013

CHAPTER 23

Restoration Days

On a beautiful, sunny Saturday afternoon in September 2008 a large crowd of members, friends and guests of the Welcome Evangelical Church gathered at the front of the building. The guests included Mr Nigel Dodds, MP for North Belfast, Mrs Dianne Dodds MEP, Mr Nelson McCausland MLA, Belfast City Councillors, local clergy and representatives of the Ulster Historical Society. Miss Tahany Hanna, the British Secretary of Amy's beloved Dohnavur Fellowship, also made a special visit to Belfast to bring greetings to the friends at the Welcome. Besides the considerable number of people standing outside the hall, many others were already seated inside waiting for the service to begin.

The occasion for which they had come together was twofold: the unveiling of an Ulster Historical Society's plaque on the front wall of the church in recognition of the work of Amy Carmichael over a hundred years earlier and the opening of the newly refurbished premises for the Welcome Evangelical Church. Pastor Jonathan Clarke announced to all present, "We are here to unveil this plaque in recognition of the work of the renowned missionary, Amy Carmichael who gave fifty years of her life to rescue and give a home to temple children in India. She also authored thirty-seven books, which have blessed thousands of people around the world. Here in Cambrai Street over a hundred years ago, Amy had the vision to start a work to reach the mill girls of that generation and that was the beginning of the Welcome Hall mission in 1889."

Mr William Humphrey, a personal friend of Pastor Jonathan Clarke, was invited to unveil the blue, circular plaque high up on the wall. The inscription simply states, "Amy Carmichael, 1867 – 1951. Missionary and Writer, ministered here 1887-1889."

After the unveiling of the tablet Jonathan announced that they had also come together to open the newly refurbished hall. He invited Mrs Ruth Carson, the oldest member of the Welcome Evangelical Church, to cut a ribbon and declare the refurbished church open to the glory of God and for public worship. Ruth prefaced her actions by saying that she hoped that future generations of young people would find the Saviour in this church as she had done eighty years earlier.

When the congregation was settled on the inside, the dedicatory service got underway with opening hymn singing, prayers and Bible readings. The Rev Jim Rea, a well-known Methodist preacher and incumbent minister at Shankill Methodist Church, spoke on behalf of the neighbouring churches.

Rev Rea expressed his satisfaction of being back at the Welcome, for to him it was like coming home, and he felt like he was standing on holy ground. Jim confessed to all present that his grandmother had been one of the shawlies for whom Amy Carmichael had originally started the work. She lived nearby in Ottawa Street, then a cobbled street with rows of small terraced houses on either side of the street. Jim told that it was at the Welcome Mission that his grandmother had been converted. She took her family to the Welcome, and it was there that Jim's mother also trusted the Lord.

Jim said that when he was a lad growing up in that area there were three famous names in religious circles: Mr Gillespie of the nearby Belfast City Mission, Frank Knox, the well-known and powerful Brethren evangelist and Mr Jack Johnston, the man who led the work at the Welcome for forty years. It was here that Jim attended the meetings with his granny and recalls how Mr Johnston engaged in evangelism. He said that back in those days, although he was not aware of it, the district might have been looked on as a slum, but Mr Johnston's work at the Hall gave the local people dignity, a sense of worth and a living experience of Jesus Christ.

Jim Rea and others always looked on the Welcome Hall as a place of local mission. Amy Carmichael and Mr Johnston in their generations were constantly reaching out into the working class community. Jim stressed that he felt the challenge was still the same today. We live in prosperous times, but all around the Welcome today are clubs and pubs, parades of people and aimless young people. They need the Gospel.

The Rev Rea also recalled that the Welcome not only had an emphasis on home missions, it was very much involved in world missions. He related that as a young boy his granny used to take him to her friend's house in Sydney Street West. Jim just called granny's friend 'Auntie Ena' and her husband was 'Uncle Joe'. Not only were Joe and Ena members of the Welcome, but Ena's brother was Jim Grainger, the missionary sent out to Africa from the Hall in the 1920s, and he spent more than fifty years in the Congo. Jim epitomised the worldwide mission and far reaching influence of the Welcome Hall.

Continuing to reminisce, Jim said that periodically he used to return to Ottawa Street and remember his days as a young boy at his granny's house. It was there that she taught him the stories of Jesus. She seemed to have such a comprehensive knowledge of the Bible. One day she said to Jim, or as she called him, "Jimmy, one day soon your granny will not be here. They will tell you that your granny is dead. Don't believe them, for then your granny, Mary McCochrane, will be more alive than ever."

Jim was grateful for that comforting aspiration expressed by his granny, for it was based on her living relationship with the risen Christ. That, with her Bible knowledge, was all due to the work of Mr Johnston and the workers of the Welcome Hall.

At the end of Jim's recollection, he stated that as a young girl, his mother-in-law also trusted Jesus Christ as Saviour at the Welcome. She used to tell how Mrs Johnston was very strict and was never reticent in speaking up about what was expected of the young people. On a certain Sunday Jim's mother-in-law and her friend, young girls at the time, arrived at the Hall wearing bright yellow straw hats. Mrs Johnston called them aside and told them that the colour of their hats was too bright for meetings at the Welcome. The two girls went home and painted their hats black, a more sober colour for the meeting. When they arrived at the next meeting the pot belly stoves were very hot with the result that very soon the rising temperature caused the paint on the hats to melt and exude a pungent smell. The hats were never worn again.

The congregation responded with laughter to that amusing story which rounded off Rev Jim Rea's recollections of his days at the Welcome Hall.

After a musical contribution by David Waugh the previous pastor, Eddie Young, spoke on behalf of the trustees of the Welcome. He congratulated and complimented Pastor Jonathan Clarke for the leadership he had shown and the ministry he exercised at the Hall. Congratulations were also conveyed to the elders and members at the Welcome for the sacrifices they had made and support for the work at the church. Eddie also recalled the great legacy the Welcome Evangelical Church enjoyed with a founder such as Miss Carmichael and a great champion of the work, Mr Jack Johnston. He reminded Pastor Clarke, the church session and all the members that the mantle of responsibility now fell on them.

David Clarke was next to speak on behalf of the elders of the church session: Eddie Young, John Walker and himself. David said that he was relatively new to the Welcome as he had only arrived as a new convert in the mid-1990s. Even in that relatively short time he had witnessed highs and lows in the history of the Welcome Evangelical Church. At the same time, David said that he believed that under the leadership of Pastor Clarke and with his excellent Bible ministry, great things lay ahead.

The late Derick Bingham, Bible teacher, evangelist and prolific author, was the invited speaker for this special occasion. Derick's book about Amy, *The Wild Bird Child*, had recently been released. He read the Scriptures to the congregation from 2 Samuel 5 and called their attention to verses 5-10: "Nevertheless David took the strong hold of Zion: the same is the city of David... And David went on, and grew great, and the Lord God of hosts was with him."

David had mustered his army to take Jerusalem, but the Jebusites had defied them and made little of David and his forces. Nevertheless, despite the odds and opposition, David took the stronghold. Derrick drew parallels from this account of David's exploits at Jerusalem and those of Amy Carmichael. Like King David, Amy also had faced her critics and despite their ridicule and disrespect, she went on to do something for God.

Derick emphasised that Amy had two great qualities in life: the ability to empathise with the needy and tenacity to endure and overcome whatever opposition or barriers she came up against. She empathised with the poor lady carrying her bundle on the Belfast Street and then had to face the censures of the well-dressed passers-by who looked on with disdain. On that day, alone with God, she surrendered her all to God and never again would she be ashamed to serve her God.

Despite the opposition she faced at the respectable Rosemary Street Church she persevered in her work, secured a site for her prefabricated hall and on it erected her tin tabernacle. Derrick related that in her notes about the despised tin tabernacle Amy remarked with a little sarcasm, "The curtains were up, the windows are in despite the croaks of the ravens."

Amy's empathy and tenacity were evident throughout her career after she left the shores of Great Britain to spend the rest of her life in India. When she exposed the abuse of young girls who were given over to the temples, her protests were met with ambivalence and contempt, but she persisted in her mission to rescue them. She was not afraid to rock the boat of the establishment when she felt her cause was right. Derick told that there were even times when Christian missionaries resented Amy's actions supposing that she was stirring a hornet's nest. Nevertheless, in spite of all these barriers that she faced and the opposition she encountered, Amy persevered in her work and won through.

The fruit of Amy's years of dedicated and single-eyed service is still evident in India. Today, the Dohnavur Fellowship, which she founded over a hundred years ago, gives refuge to Indian children who are in moral and physical danger, operates a hospital where 36,000 outpatients are attended to each year and has a school for Indian missionaries' children from twenty-three Indian states.

The fruit of that ministry is still evident in the continuing work and witness of the Welcome Evangelical Church, which she founded when she erected that first building on Cambrai Street. They just called it, "Amy's Tin Tabernacle".

CHAPTER 24

Give me the Faith

One hundred twenty-five years have passed since a youthful Amy Carmichael opened her "Tin Tabernacle" on Cambrai Street in North Belfast. After a short while in England, this unique servant of God gave another fifty years of her life to rescuing babies and children, especially young girls, from situations and backgrounds of extreme danger and providing them with a safe home. It was for that reason she founded the Dohnavur Fellowship in South India in 1901.

On 4th October 1931, Amy was badly injured in a fall, which left her confined to bed until her death in 1951. During those twenty years Amy, always a prolific writer and a poet, used much of her time to continue to put pen to paper and produce her thirty-seven published books, some of which have become Christian classics with a worldwide readership. After a full life of service for her Lord, Amy, surrounded by her beloved children at her Dohnavur Home, went to be with the Saviour she had loved and served so well on earth.

Amy not only left an immense legacy of blessing by founding the Welcome Hall to reach the lost and underprivileged in Belfast and establishing the Dohnavur Fellowship for the rescue of children in India, she also left an imprint of Bible principles which governed her life and guided her work for more than sixty years. These principles of faith, love, devotion, vision, compassion and mission helped her accomplish her goals.

These same guiding values were first established in Amy's life when she was arrested by the words that came to her that drab Sunday morning at the water fountain in Belfast. Out of the grey mist she perceived a voice reminding her: "Gold, silver, precious stones, wood, hay, stubble, every man's work shall be made manifest for the Day shall declare it, because it shall be tried by fire, and the fire shall try every man's work of what sort it is. If any man's work abide…" Later that day, alone with God in her Belfast home, Amy resolved to live only for God for the rest of her days.

Although Amy never returned to Belfast, the qualities and values, which governed her personal life, set a pattern for the whole future of the work at the Welcome Hall.

Many of Amy Carmichael's poems not only sum up her life of dedicated and sacrificial service but also demonstrated the standards which were required of Miss Mitchell, Jack Johnston and a succession of pastors who dedicated their lives to maintain the witness at the Welcome Hall during the past 125 years.

When Miss Mitchell had to step up to a leadership role at the Welcome Hall after the departure of Amy to England she had to forgo many of the luxuries of silken selfishness to give the remaining years of her life to work among the underprivileged girls on the Shankill.

From subtle love of softening things,
From easy choices, weakening,
(Not thus are spirits fortified,
Not this way went the Crucified)

From all that dims Thy Calvary
O Lamb of God, deliver me.

In 1926 when Jack Johnston, encouraged by his wife Elizabeth, answered the challenge of Canon Warren, the godly rector at St Silas Church of Ireland, to open the neglected premises which had been Amy's Welcome Hall for the furtherance of the Gospel, instead of fearing when he should aspire, or faltering when he should climb higher, Jack stood up as a soldier of Jesus Christ to follow his Master.

At that time Amy was in India, far away from the hustle and bustle of life on the Shankill, but she wrote words which suited Jack Johnston's step of faith:

Strength of my heart, I need not fail,
Not mine to fear but to obey,
With such a Leader, who could quail?
Thou art as Thou wert yesterday.
Strength of my heart, I rest in Thee,
Fulfill Thy purposes through me.

After years of missionary service in Liberia, West Africa, in 1964 Robert and Isobel Mackey accepted an invitation to pastor the Welcome Hall. During his five years of service in North Belfast they were not sheltered from fierce winds of adversity. Northern Ireland was plunged into one of the most tumultuous periods in its history. Rows of terraced houses were torched or bombed. Families were evacuated from their houses. People were afraid to venture any distance from their homes. Little children were terrified. Those were not days of easy choices. Through it all Pastor Mackey did not diminish his clear presentation of the Gospel and deliverance from sin through Christ the Lamb of God.

From prayer that asks that I may be
Sheltered from winds that beat on Thee,
From fearing when I should aspire,
From faltering when I should climb higher
From silken self, O Captain, free
Thy soldier who would follow Thee.

Eddie Young and his brother Harry were boxers of considerable note in their younger days. They had the scars to prove it. Both brothers were associated with the Welcome Evangelical Church since 1949. Harry and his wife Joann, were sent from the Welcome Hall to spend the rest of their lives taking the Gospel to Muslims in various parts of the world.

Meanwhile, Eddie and Sadie Young were also sent from the Welcome and for twenty years they served God in Senegal, West Africa, as missionaries with the Worldwide Evangelization Crusade. After those very productive years in West Africa Eddie accepted an invitation to be the pastor of his home church. Eddie was inducted as pastor of the Welcome Evangelical Church in 1980, a ministry he and Sadie maintained until his retirement in 1997. Even then, during subsequent pastoral vacancies Eddie was on hand to continue to help in the ministry of the Word of God at the Welcome. During his seventeen years as pastor at the Welcome Hall many mission halls in the surrounding area were forced to close down due to redevelopment and reallocation of the population. Through it all Eddie maintained a constant witness to the Gospel and made sure that the Welcome Hall survived in times of shifting loyalties and shrinking spiritual commitment.

Any scars Eddie has to show from his years as a teenage boxer are not to be compared with the invisible marks on his life after sixty years in Christian service. Amy asked the question, "Can we follow the Saviour far, who have no wound or scar?" Perhaps those scar marks on Eddie's life find a parallel in this famous poem that Amy Carmichael penned in India:

Hast thou no scar?
No hidden scar on foot, or side, or hand?
I hear thee sung as mighty in the land,
I hear them hail thy bright ascendant star,
Hast thou no scar?

Hast thou no wound?
Yet, I was wounded by the archers, spent.
Leaned me against the tree to die, and rent
By ravening beasts that compassed me, I swooned:
Hast thou no wound?

No wound? No scar?
Yet as the Master shall the servant be,
And pierced are the feet that follow Me;
But thine are whole. Can he have followed far
Who has no wound nor scar?

Jonathan Clarke is the incumbent pastor at Welcome Evangelical Church and has been since May 2006. He and the congregation at the Welcome face a new era of great challenges, challenges that are very different from those which Amy encountered at the end of the nineteenth century, situations completely different from those pastors who have gone before him. Nevertheless, Jonathan shares and lives by the principles and values which governed and guided Amy Carmichael 125 years ago: faith in God, devotion to His church, vision for the work, compassion for the lost and a sense of mission to accomplish God's purpose at the Welcome.

Amy put it best in her poem:

Give me the Love that leads the way
The Faith that nothing can dismay
The Hope no disappointments tire
The Passion that'll burn like fire
Let me not sink to be a clod
Make me Thy fuel, Flame of God.

Most of Amy's poems are published in the CLC book "Mountain Breezes"

CHAPTER 25

Principles and Poems

On an inclement Sunday morning on a city-centre street a teenage Amy Carmichael had a reality check about the true values of life. The words of the Apostle Paul came tumbling into her mind, "Gold, silver, precious stones, wood, hay, stubble, every man's work shall be made manifest for the Day shall declare it, because it shall be tried by fire, and the fire shall try every man's work of what sort it is. If any man's work abide..." This "day" to which Paul referred was the day for which Amy resolved to live and these true eternal values would guide and govern her long and productive life.

These values were always evident in her poems and writings:

Love
Many crowd the Saviour's Kingdom,
Few receive His Cross,
Many seek His consolation,
Few will suffer loss
For the dear sake of the Master,
Counting all but dross.

Many sit at Jesus› table,
Few will fast with Him
When the sorrow-cup of anguish
Trembles to the brim.

Few watch with Him in the garden
Who have sung the hymn.
 Many will confess His wisdom.
Few embrace his shame,
Many, should He smile upon them,
Will His praise proclaim;
Then, if for a while He leave them,
They desert his Name.

But the souls who love Him truly
In woe or in sweet bliss,
These will count their truest heart›s blood
Not their own, but His;
Saviour, Thou Who thus hast loved me,
Give me love like this.

Faith
"Thou art the Lord who slept upon the pillow,
Thou art the Lord who soothed the furious sea,
What matters beating wind and tossing billow
If only we are in the boat with Thee?

Hold us quiet through the age-long minute
While Thou art silent and the wind is shrill :
Can the boat sink while Thou, dear Lord, are in it;
Can the heart faint that waiteth on Thy will?"
Amy Carmichael

Devotion

"Hereby perceive we the love of God, because He laid down His life for us, and we ought to lay down our lives for the brethren." How often I think of that 'ought.' No sugary sentiment there. Just the stern, glorious trumpet call, OUGHT. But can words tell the joy buried deep within? Mine cannot. It laughs at words."

Amy Carmichael in Christian-living, sacrifice

"God Hold us to that which drew us first, when the Cross was the attraction, and we wanted nothing else."

Amy Carmichael, in *Gods Missionary*

Vision

The tom-toms thumped straight on all night, and the darkness shuddered round me like a living, feeling thing. I could not go to sleep, so I lay awake and looked, and I saw, as it seemed, this:

That I stood on a grassy sward, and at my feet a precipice broke sheer down into infinite space. I looked, but saw no bottom; only cloud shapes, black and furiously coiled, and great shadow-shrouded hollows, and unfathomable depths. Back I drew, dizzy at the depth.

Then I saw forms of people moving single file along the grass. They were making for the edge. There was a woman with a baby in her arms and another little child holding onto her dress. She was on the very verge. Then I saw that she was blind. She lifted her foot for the next step... it trod air. She was over, and the children over with her. Oh, the cry as they went over!

Then I saw more streams of people flowing from all quarters. All were blind, stone blind; all made straight for the precipice edge.

There were shrieks, as they suddenly knew themselves falling, and a tossing up of helpless arms, catching, clutching at empty air. But some went over quietly, and fell without a sound.

Then I wondered, with a wonder that was simply agony, why no one stopped them at the edge. I could not. I was glued to the ground, and I could only call; though I strained and tried, only whispers would come.

Then I saw that along the edge there were sentries set at intervals. But the intervals were too great; there were wide, unguarded gaps between. And over these gaps the people fell in their blindness, quite unwarned; and the green grass seemed blood-red to me, and the gulf yawned like the mouth of hell.

Then I saw, like a little picture of peace, a group of people under some trees with their backs turned toward the gulf. They were making daisy chains. Sometimes when a piercing shriek cut the quiet air and reached them, it disturbed them and they thought it a rather vulgar noise. And if one of their number started up and wanted to go and do something to help, then all the others would pull that one down. "Why should you get so excited about it? You must wait for a definite call to go! You haven't finished your daisy chain yet. It would be really selfish," they said, "to leave us to finish the work alone."

There was another group. It was made up of people whose great desire was to get more sentries out; but they found that very few wanted to go, and sometimes there were no sentries set for miles and miles of the edge.

Once a girl stood alone in her place, waving the people back; but her mother and other relations called and reminded her that her furlough was due; she must not break the rules. And being tired and needing a change, she had to go and rest for awhile; but no one was sent to guard her gap, and over and over the people fell, like a waterfall of souls.

Once a child caught at a tuft of grass that grew at the very brink of the gulf; it clung convulsively, and it called-but nobody seemed to hear. Then the roots of the grass gave way, and with a cry the child went over, its two little hands still holding tight to the torn-off bunch of grass. And the girl who longed to be back in her gap thought she heard the little one cry, and she sprang up and wanted to go; at which they reproved her, reminding her that noone is necessary anywhere; the gap would be well taken care of, they knew. And then they sang a hymn.

Then through the hymn came another sound like the pain of a million broken hearts wrung out in one full drop, one sob. And a horror of great darkness was upon me, for I knew what it was--the Cry of the Blood.

Then thundered a voice, the voice of the Lord. "And He said, 'What hast thou done, The voice of thy brother's blood crieth unto me from the ground.'"

The tom-toms still beat heavily, the darkness still shuddered and shivered about me; I heard the yells of the devil-dancers and weird, wild shriek of the devil-possessed just outside the gate.

What does it matter, after all? It has gone on for years; it will go on for years. Why make such a fuss about it?

God forgive us! God arouse us! Shame us out of our callousness! Shame us out of our sin!

Compassion

"If souls can suffer alongside, and I hardly know it, because the spirit of discernment is not in me, then I know nothing of Calvary love."

Amy Carmichael,

Mission

"It is more important that you should know about the reverses than about the successes of the war. We shall have all eternity to celebrate the victories, but we have only the few hours before sunset in which to win them. We are not winning them as we should, because the fact of the reverses is so little realized, and the needed reinforcements are not forthcoming, as they would be in the position were thoroughly understood... So we have tried to tell you the truth: the uninteresting, unromantic truth."

Amy Carmichael

"There have been times of late when I have had to hold on to one text with all my might: 'It is required in stewards that a man may be found faithful.' Praise God, it does not say 'successful'."

Amy Carmichael in *Faithfulness*

"Hereby perceive we the love of God, because He laid down His life for us, and we ought to lay down our lives for the brethren." How often I think of that 'ought.' No sugary sentiment there. Just the stern, glorious trumpet call, OUGHT. But can words tell the joy buried deep within? Mine cannot. It laughs at words."

Amy Carmichael